Difficult Conversations
In A Week

Martin Manser

Martin Manser is an expert communicator with a unique combination of skills and experience. He has compiled or edited over 200 reference books on the English language, Bible reference and business skills in a 30-year professional career. He is an English-language specialist and teaches English to business colleagues: participants in his courses find them to be a safe place to ask questions and for participants' confidence to grow. Since 2002 he has also been a Language Consultant and Trainer, leading courses in business communications for national and international companies and organizations on language learning, report writing, project management and time management.

Difficult Conversations

Martin Manser

www.inaweek.co.uk

Teach
Yourself®

First published in Great Britain in 2014 by Hodder & Stoughton. An Hachette UK company.

First published in US in 2014 by The McGraw-Hill Companies, Inc.

This edition published 2014

Typeset by Cenveo® Publisher Services.

Printed and bound in Great Britain by CPI Group (UK) Ltd., Croydon, CRO 4YY.

Hodder & Stoughton policy is to use papers that are natural, renewable and recyclable products and made from wood grown in sustainable forests. The logging and manufacturing processes are expected to conform to the environmental regulations of the country of origin.

Hodder & Stoughton Ltd

338 Euston Road

London NW1 3BH

www.hodder.co.uk

Contents

Acknowledgments

I wish to thank Linda Eley for her careful typing of my manuscript and Michael Allmey for his helpful contribution.

Martin Manser

Note: This book is not intended to replace legal advice on handling HR issues at work. For matters relating to the law, consult your HR department.

Introduction

How do you deal professionally with a colleague whose work is seriously below standard? A supplier who is always late? Saying 'no' graciously? Giving someone bad news?

Many of us have been on the receiving end of business conversations that have been badly handled, poorly timed or scarcely prepared for by the person we're talking to. We may say, 'How could they have treated me like this after all I have done for them?' Many colleagues feel undervalued at the way their bosses deal with them. This practical book offers help to new and aspiring managers in a variety of business situations, such as delivering bad news in an appraisal, and how to work with a range of colleagues who may be lazy, negative or incompetent.

In this book we'll explore the following:

Sunday: Why are some conversations difficult? We may tend to avoid difficult conversations: how else can you deal with them?

Monday: Manage your emotions Distinguish the facts of an incident and how colleagues feel about it and their sense of identity.

Tuesday: Prepare well The venue, atmosphere and timing of a difficult conversation are all important. It is essential that you prepare well, especially your opening words and the direction that you want the conversation to go in, including alternative ways to resolve the issue.

Wednesday: Listen carefully As you listen, you discover more about your colleague's background and motivation. You also need to learn how to ask incisive questions that get to the root of an issue.

Thursday: Treat colleagues with respect In a difficult conversation, you need to affirm your colleague and continue to listen until they feel heard. You will explain your point of view politely, yet firmly, being neither passive nor aggressive in tone.

Friday: Seek change Involve colleagues in a conversation; learn how to deal with certain kinds of colleagues, for example, those who are lazy, aggressive or shy.

Saturday: Build trusting relationships Work hard to develop strong working relationships, so that when you have to have a difficult conversation, you will be better placed to do so because you will know the person better.

Each day of the week covers a different area and the material is structured by beginning with an introduction to show what the day is about. Then comes the main material which explains the key lessons by clarifying important principles that are backed up by tips, case studies, etc. Each day concludes with a summary, follow-up and multiple-choice questions, to reinforce the learning points.

The principles I outline here are the fruit of over 30 years in business, particularly in the area of communications, and over ten years in leading courses on business communications. As I have reflected on participants' responses to the workshops I have led, two comments keep recurring: 'You gave me more confidence' and 'The workshop was a refresher course.' My hope therefore is that as you read and act on what I have written, it will be a refresher course that will give you fresh confidence to tackle difficult conversations at work.

Martin Manser

Why are some conversations difficult?

Introduction

Today, we plunge straight into the issue of difficult conversations with a story about dealing with a colleague whose work has become unsatisfactory. The story raises a range of different points:

- the tendency to avoid dealing with a difficult issue
- the need to explore options in a positive and constructive way rather than negatively and destructively
- the need to manage emotions, listen well and treat people with respect.

These matters form the foundation for topics that we will consider throughout the rest of the week.

We will also look at:

- why we tend to avoid difficult conversations
- other ways in which we deal with difficult conversations
- different kinds of sensitive issues that we encounter at work
- self-awareness and how a model can be applied to develop better working relationships
- the need to focus on the goal in pursuing a difficult conversation.

SUNDAY
MONDAY
TUESDAY
WEDNESDAY
THURSDAY
FRIDAY
SATURDAY

Why do we avoid tackling sensitive issues?

Gary was a competent and well-meaning salesman, but he had been in that role for too long. He had become complacent with his customers and too dependent on his support team. He preferred to be in the office being disruptive rather than generating sales. Gary's manager, John, spent some time wondering what to do, but he delayed taking action as he didn't like confrontation.

Recognizing Gary's skills, John eventually managed to identify another sales job in the organization where his expertise would be valued, but in an unfamiliar environment that would challenge him and give him a fresh start. So, with the agreement of the Sales Manager of the new role, John called Gary in for a meeting.

At first the conversation did not go well. As anticipated, Gary became defensive, sensing a personal attack and some hidden agenda to replace him. John quickly realized there was no point focusing on the negatives, and so instead invited Gary to outline the parts of his role that he enjoyed, and then those he found tedious. John and Gary were eventually even able to agree on some aspects of his work that were difficult and probably could be done better.

Building on this discussion, John was then able to focus on the areas Gary did enjoy and was successful in, and began to highlight parallels with the needs within other parts of the organization.

Gary liked intrigue, and so John let slip that he had heard that another team was looking for an experienced salesman, He went on to say that he thought Gary would be a great fit for the role. John wondered aloud whether Gary would be interested in him finding out more and putting feelers out on his behalf.

After some thought and minor push-back about the risk of change, Gary agreed that actually this could be an exciting possibility.

That conversation was eight years ago and Gary is now Regional Sales Manager for Europe and Far East, having had a successful and enjoyable career in the new team.

John often considered whether he had pushed the limits of honesty, or just acted as a good manager. On balance, he decided that by understanding Gary's motivations, the needs of the company and by looking constructively for active solutions to the problem, he was able to turn a confrontational situation into one of mentoring and career development, which certainly helped him and supported the company.

This story touches on several themes that we will discuss as we move through this week. Let's look first at why we tend to avoid tackling sensitive issues. Here are several reasons why we avoid such matters:

- You deny there is a difficulty at all.
- You don't know what to say or where to begin.
- You don't want to hurt the other person's feelings, so you say nothing.
- You want people to like you and raising an issue with them might disturb that relationship.
- You know that such a conversation will be stressful for you and that it may place more demands on you than you can bear, so it is simpler just to leave it.
- You don't know how the other person will react. Might they lose their temper and suddenly express their feelings strongly and forcefully? How would you react if they burst into tears? What would you do if your comments met with silence? Rather than face an uncertain response, you decide to do nothing.
- You think that your well-intentioned actions might be perceived as bullying, treating them with contempt, so you follow the proverb 'it is better safe than sorry' and do not take any risks at all.
- You think that tackling one issue might open up even more complex, and possibly awkward and unpleasant, matters, so you decide that it is better to leave well alone.
- You have raised such issues with other colleagues before and discussions have gone badly: your intentions were

misinterpreted and your motives questioned. The whole matter was so unpleasant that you decided never to try to deal with such delicate matters again.

● You do not have a good trusting relationship with the person concerned.

NO NO, YOUR WORK RECORD IS EXCELLENT, IT'S JUST THAT ...

However, if you avoid an issue and do not deal with it, it will probably only get worse. Both the other person's behaviour and your feelings may take deeper root and become increasingly firmly established. Your frustration and emotional stress may become so intense as you keep your feelings in that you might express your anger forcefully at the smallest thing the other person does. It's like toothache that does not get better but becomes more painful, or like a rattle in your car that does not disappear but becomes louder. Sooner or later, you have to deal with it.

 TIP *If you avoid an issue and don't deal with it, it will probably get worse.*

Other ways of dealing with a difficult conversation

Here are some other ways of dealing with a difficult conversation:

- competing, where one side firmly imposes their will, often in a domineering way, not being concerned with others' feelings
- accommodating, where the main aim is to maintain the relationship at all costs, and please and satisfy the wishes of others
- compromising, where you agree a solution that is halfway between what each side wants, with each side giving up something. The different sides negotiate and agree that one side 'wins' on some matters while the other side 'wins' on others
- collaborating, where the different sides take time to work effectively together to develop solutions that satisfy both sides.

Note that in certain situations, each of these styles might be appropriate. For example, a competing style could be appropriate if you are asking for a refund when you return faulty goods to a shop. You are not concerned with the shop assistant's feelings: you are in the right to seek a refund. An accommodating style might be appropriate when the relationship is far more important than the relatively unimportant issue being considered. A compromising style might be appropriate when dealing with a relatively minor matter when there is little time to sit down and agree a well-thought-out solution.

In this book, we will pursue the collaborating approach, taking time to listen to and respect the other person and creatively seek a solution.

What are the different kinds of sensitive issues?

What kinds of sensitive issues are we discussing? Here are some examples:

- a colleague's work is unsatisfactory and as manager you need to discuss that in an appraisal
- matters concerning pay and conditions. For example, after several months in one job, I discovered that a colleague with similar background, qualifications and experience to me was being paid more than me. I felt unfairly treated
- making a colleague redundant
- dealing with colleagues who are negative, disruptive or argumentative
- working with a boss who intimidates
- working with a boss who is weak
- working with a boss who keeps on giving you more and more work and then watches over you to make sure you do it in the way they want
- working with colleagues whose behaviour or hygiene is inappropriate
- working with colleagues whose work is constantly delivered late.

Self-awareness

Let's stand back at this point and instead of continuing to look at the other person, let's look at the wider matter of self-awareness. How well do you really know yourself?

The framework of the 'Johari window' is helpful here. It is a graphic model that is widely used to promote improved understanding in corporate environments and in self-help groups. It is based on a window divided into four panes representing the four types of personal awareness: open, hidden, blind and unknown. The Johari window is named after *Jo*seph Luft and *Harry* Ingham, the American psychologists who developed it in 1955.

Known to yourself	Not known to yourself
1 open area	2 blind area
3 hidden area	4 unknown area
Known to others	Not known to others

1 is the open area, known by yourself and known to others, such as your skills, knowledge and experience. It is good to increase the size of this area to facilitate effective work and good co-operation.

2 is the area that is known by others in a group but unknown to you: you are blind to it. This could be a character trait or personal feelings of rejection or inadequacy, which others notice but can be difficult for people themselves to accept and work through. It is good to receive feedback in this area in a sensitive, non-judgemental way so that an individual's self-knowledge can increase.

3 is the area that is known to yourself but that you keep hidden from others, so they do not know. Some of this information is very personal (for example, insecurities and private fears) and it is natural to keep these hidden, but other aspects, which may relate to skills or experience that could be applied to work, can usefully be disclosed to help an individual and group work more effectively together. While the general practices of a company or organization may encourage or hinder self-disclosure, how much an individual actually

chooses to reveal about themselves is ultimately at that person's own discretion.

4 is the area of abilities, feelings and experience that are unknown to both the individual and also others. Examples are abilities or skills that someone does not know they have.

The significance of this model is to increase the size of 1, the open area. You do this by gradually disclosing more of the hidden area (i.e. decreasing the size of area 3). Doing this gradually is important and something you do all the time in building a relationship, for example, you don't open up about everything in your life when you meet someone for the first time, but do so slowly over a period of time. For example, when you discover that a colleague went to the same university as you, you ask if they knew certain lecturers in the department. If you and they both remember the lecturer, you may comment on your perception of that lecturer and your opinion of their work. Such discussion is a step in deepening your relationship with your colleague.

The other key area of personal growth is to accept feedback from others, to minimize area 2, the blind area, so that you learn things about yourself that are clear to others but that you are not aware of. However, such feedback must be given in a sensitive way.

Focus on the goal

Let's conclude today by focusing on what we want to achieve in a difficult conversation. Our aim is to help people grow, so that each colleague can achieve their full potential. We want to resolve a matter, not for it to develop into conflict with both sides voicing their opinions and blaming each other.

Here are some guidelines:

● Distinguish between the facts of what happened and the feelings surrounding the incident. Think back to an incident in your life when something bad happened to you. There was the incident itself, and also the emotions surrounding the incident. For example, when I discovered that I was being paid less than the colleague who was doing the same work as me

SO, NO BEATING ABOUT THE BUSH — SOMEBODY DEFINITELY OUGHT TO DO SOMETHING, AND SOONISH

SUNDAY

MONDAY

TUESDAY

WEDNESDAY

THURSDAY

FRIDAY

SATURDAY

when she came from a similar background and had similar skills and experience, there was the issue itself of the pay but also the emotions of anger and feeling unimportant and undervalued. Sometimes after we have dealt with the facts, the unpleasant effects from the incident remain, or as we say, 'we are left with a bad taste in our mouth' (for more on emotions, see Monday).

- Prepare well for a difficult conversation, for example regarding the venue, the timing and your opening words (for more on this, see Tuesday).
- Listen to others in order to build up a fuller understanding of the reasons for someone's behaviour. Often, we make false assumptions about colleagues' actions, intentions, etc., because we are missing some crucial piece of information. As you listen to others, you may discover the real focus of what you need to be discussing, which might be different from what you originally thought (for more on this see Wednesday).
- Realize people's sense of identity is affected, hence their defensiveness and feeling threatened (for more on this see Wednesday and Thursday).
- Continue to respect and value people as individuals. Most people feel undervalued at work and many managers could do much more to value their staff (for more on this see Thursday).

● Remain focused. Your aim is not to win an argument: that would mean your colleague would have to lose, which is unlikely to be acceptable. What you want is to achieve a clear outcome and where possible continue a good working relationship with your colleague (for more on this see Friday).

Remember, your aim isn't to win an argument, but to achieve a clear outcome and continue to build a good working relationship.

The e2c2 feedback model

Jo was a new manager and felt she was suddenly faced with a very difficult situation when her colleague Ray was late in delivering his month-end report. Jo found it helpful to follow her boss's advice in using the e2c2 model (e2c2 stands for 'evidence; effect; change; continue'). She spoke to Ray, giving him the **evidence** clearly: 'Your report was three days late,' adding the **effect** this had on other colleagues: 'The delay meant that other departments had to make estimates based on inaccurate data.'

By understanding the specific facts about what he had done wrong, and its impact on others, Ray realized his error, so he was ready for Jo when she went on with the necessary **change**: 'It would be very helpful if your next report – due in two weeks' time – were to be completed punctually.' Ray knew he should **continue** to concentrate on his time-management skills to be an effective member of Jo's team. By using the e2c2 feedback model, Jo helped Ray in a positive way.

Summary

Today we've looked at:

- an example of dealing with a sensitive issue
- what sensitive issues typically arise at work
- reasons for our tendency to avoid dealing with sensitive issues
- ways in which difficult conversations can be tackled, apart from avoiding the issue
- the 'Johari window' model representing different types of personal awareness. In particular we saw that to promote personal growth and more effective working relationships, two areas can be developed:
  – receive feedback, in a sensitive way, on areas that others know but you are unaware of
  – disclose more of yourself, your skills, experience, etc. gradually, to others to facilitate stronger working relationships
- the need to focus positively on the goal, for example by listening to others, respecting them and preparing well for meetings.

Follow-up

1 What difficult conversations are you avoiding at work?

2 What sensitive issues have arisen in your professional career? How have you and your colleagues handled these? In what ways do you think they could have been handled better?

3 What knowledge, skills and experience do you have that you could disclose more to your colleagues? When will you do this?

MONDAY

TUESDAY

WEDNESDAY

THURSDAY

FRIDAY

SATURDAY

Questions

1. Dealing with sensitive issues is:
   a) difficult, so I avoid doing so ❏
   b) important, and that is why I'm reading this book ❏
   c) a waste of time ❏
   d) unnecessary. ❏

2. If I don't deal with a significant issue at work:
   a) I know it will get worse, so I need to tackle it ❏
   b) I hope it will go away ❏
   c) I hope someone else will ❏
   d) it might just get better by itself. ❏

3. I deal with difficult conversations by:
   a) giving in to others' demands; I just want a quiet life ❏
   b) losing my temper ❏
   c) acting aggressively and forcefully exerting my authority ❏
   d) listening to both sides, respecting individuals and seeking a creative solution. ❏

4. Solving an issue by compromising is:
   a) never appropriate ❏
   b) always appropriate ❏
   c) appropriate when the matter is relatively minor and time is short ❏
   d) appropriate when no one is right, but you don't say that. ❏

5. The model 'Johari window' shows:
   a) a way of making decisions ❏
   b) areas that are or are not known to ourselves and are or are not known to others ❏
   c) a way of training new members of staff ❏
   d) a new kind of double glazing. ❏

6. How much an individual opens up about their own self:
   a) is at the discretion of the individual ❏
   b) can be forced by aggressive management styles ❏
   c) depends only on their background ❏
   d) sorry, what are you talking about? ❏

7. In our company or organization, feedback should be given:
   a) negatively ❏
   b) insensitively ❏
   c) constructively ❏
   d) spontaneously. ❏

8. In our company or organization, we aim for each colleague to:
   a) go home punctually at 5p.m. ❏
   b) achieve their full potential ❏
   c) become patient and knowledgeable ❏
   d) become confident and extrovert. ❏

9. When dealing with a sensitive issue, my aim is to:
a) win at all costs ❏
b) discuss several different options but keep the outcomes vague ❏
c) get home as soon as possible ❏
d) achieve a clear outcome and maintain the working relationship with the colleague concerned. ❏

10. In the e2c2 model, e and c stand for:
a) economics, emotions, culture, communication ❏
b) evidence, effect, change, continue ❏
c) ethics, eye contact, character, criticism ❏
d) empowering, empathy, confidence, conflict. ❏

MONDAY

Manage your emotions

Introduction

I like trains. If I am leading a workshop or giving a presentation elsewhere, I prefer travelling by train to driving my car as the train gives me time to think and read. But, as with any aspect of life, events happen that are outside our control. Twice I've been on trains that have been severely delayed because of suicides. It's interesting to see how we as passengers react. All too easily, the initial thoughts that I and my fellow passengers have are ones of anger at the inconvenience caused by the delay as the emergency services and railway authorities have to do their work. When I've found myself becoming angry, however, I have had to make myself think of the victim and their family: their experience must surely be far more intense than mine.

The point I'm making is this: we cannot always control what happens to us in life, but we can control our emotional response to such events.

Today, we look at the area of managing our emotions in difficult conversations:

- don't ignore feelings
- recognize your own emotional make-up
- manage your thoughts
- do express feelings
- affirm a sense of identity
- don't blame, but reframe.

Don't ignore feelings

As we noted yesterday, it is helpful to distinguish the incident – what happened – from the feelings, for example of anger or hurt, about the incident itself.

In difficult conversations, we cannot ignore feelings because they are important. People *feel* they want to be listened to; colleagues *feel* undervalued and want to be recognized.

However, we sense that to allow feelings to be aired could become complex and confused – anything might happen. People might well get hurt; relationships could be deeply affected. It is here that somehow we need to include feelings, because if we don't allow them to be expressed they will surface later, perhaps in ways that will not be helpful. So, feelings need to be expressed. If we don't express them, our anger may build up. How then can feelings be expressed in as safe a way as possible?

TIP *Distinguish an issue and the feelings of anger or hurt surrounding the issue.*

Recognize your own emotional make-up

Different cultures express emotions differently. I have some African friends who tend to be exuberant. I'm British and I'm not very emotional. I cry rarely. I'm normally fairly even-tempered. Generally, life is a steady course but I do have emotions, and these surface from time to time. I feel great sadness and anger at the many injustices in the world. I become angry when I see resources of time and money being wasted.

Looking back, my parents did not often express their feelings towards each other. Maybe they were of that generation. We didn't generally discuss emotions as a family – what counted were events. So I am having to learn to handle that part of my life: to accept feelings as part of a natural and healthy life.

So it can be helpful to think: what is your emotional make-up? What is your attitude to your emotions? Which emotions do you find easy to express? Which are more difficult?

SUNDAY

MONDAY

TUESDAY

WEDNESDAY

THURSDAY

FRIDAY

SATURDAY

It is here that we sometimes go wrong. We are surrounded by the claims that 'Real men don't cry', that it is wrong to feel anger or express fears, but we cannot always have strong feelings of happiness.

I find it helpful to write down my feelings and also explore them with my wife and some trusted friends. In that way, I can usually see their significance and can be helped to move on.

Sometimes our feelings spill over into judgements about others. For example, we may help someone a lot over many years but they never thank us. Our anger may burst out in the form of a judgement: 'You only think about yourself all the time, never anyone else.' Note that this is different from a statement about our feelings, which might be, 'I feel hurt. I thought we were friends.'

Manage your thoughts

The way in which we can manage our feelings is to manage our thoughts. Remember that emotions are not thoughts. Our thoughts are often unfocused or unclear. For example, a few years ago I was convinced that birds were flying in the loft area of our house and I could hear them every morning as I lay in bed. A friend who repairs roofs came round and he assured me that that was not so – there were no holes in the roof for them to enter and they were simply flying onto the roof itself. I needed to be told the truth – and I had to let that factual truth affect my thoughts and then let my thoughts affect my feelings of insecurity.

Applying this to a relationship with another person, my feelings towards a friend needed to be affected by the truth. One day I unintentionally ignored a friend as she passed me in the street. My friend thought I had intentionally ignored her and wondered aloud what she had done to upset me. I needed to explain I simply had not seen her.

Challenge assumptions

We have feelings, which are based on certain thoughts. These thoughts are in turn based on certain assumptions. So we may need to challenge such assumptions to see if they are really true. If they turn out to be false, we can change our thoughts. (My assumptions about birds in our loft were based on the fact that there might well be holes in the roof, so I tested that, found it to be wrong and had to change my thoughts.)

In a difficult conversation, we tend to make assumptions about the intentions of the other party. However, we see and hear only what a person is doing and saying, not the intentions behind what they have done or said. For example, who can know what is in the mind of a colleague who is behaving inappropriately towards a member of the opposite sex? We cannot discern what is in the other person's mind; we only know what is in our own.

If someone is an hour late for work every day and always blames it on the transport system, we may be kind and treat that colleague as if they are telling the truth although we are not sure they are. Or we may be firmer and suggest over a period of time they change their behaviour.

In order to challenge assumptions about others' intentions, we need to uncover what their intentions are. A clear, neutral, moderate statement such as 'I realize that I don't really know how you see this matter' can be a way to open up a conversation to its next stage. Acknowledging that you do not understand someone else's intentions – and that you are committed to understanding them and their views – can be a significant step forward in encouraging a colleague to express and articulate their intentions.

SUNDAY

MONDAY

TUESDAY

WEDNESDAY

THURSDAY

FRIDAY

SATURDAY

TIP *Acknowledge that you are committed to understanding your colleague's intentions and views.*

Express emotions

Earlier today, we discussed the need not to ignore emotions. But we need to do more: we need to express them. Here I think it is helpful to see expressing feelings as one stage and solving the problem as a later stage. So, if someone loses their temper and is allowed to express themselves freely for a few minutes, that clears the air and they will probably feel better. We must resist the temptation to try to stop someone in the middle of expressing their anger but allow them to release that and then move on from that.

As we allow people to air their own opinions and express deep emotions, the result can – if managed well – be that some long-standing issues can be resolved, leading to stronger working relationships.

I was at a secular 'Training trainers' seminar a few years ago. At the beginning we were asked to say why we were there. I thought, 'I'll never see these people again, so I might as well be honest,' and so said, 'I'm afraid that people will ask me questions I don't know the answers to.' Maybe encouraged by my honest and open sharing of my feelings, the next participant, Fay, said that she had been recently promoted to the role of training manager and that her boss had told her she had got her job because of some good luck and a lot of sticky tape (it seemed that her boss wondered whether she had the capabilities to fulfil the role). I immediately sensed that what this lady needed was not a few hints on becoming a better trainer but a far deeper affirmation of her role.

The conference was a two-day event and nervously (after checking with the course leader) at the beginning of the second day I presented Fay with a white lily with the words, 'On behalf of the group, I would like to affirm you as a trainer.' She was significantly moved. By Fay expressing her feelings and my listening and responding to her, she was helped significantly and able to develop as a person.

Acknowledge emotions

After feelings have been expressed, it is important to acknowledge them, perhaps by saying, 'I didn't know you felt that way.' Acknowledging the expression of feelings is an important step because in so doing you are affirming your appreciation of the other person's feelings. For more on affirming others, see below and Thursday.

Affirm a sense of identity

Look back at the story of the beginning of Sunday.

At first the conversation did not go well. As anticipated, Gary sensed a personal attack and some hidden agenda to replace him.

When we criticize someone, for example, for the poor quality of their work, they may feel threatened and become defensive. They may start to justify themselves, reminding us of all their good aspects of their work. Moreover, when our work is criticized, it is not just our work that is affected; deep within us we feel threatened and our sense of identify may be damaged.

In that opening story on Sunday, Gary felt inwardly hurt and confused. We have probably all known such feelings. After giving a brief presentation a few years ago, a colleague told me that my work was 'not professional'. I was surprised, hurt and confused. My self-image was challenged and my sense of self-worth was attacked.

If our identity is attacked, we feel insecure and may begin to believe what is being said about our character, skills or knowledge: 'Maybe I am no good, after all.' Here we need to think realistically about ourselves – we are neither perfect in every way nor extremely incompetent. We need to manage our thoughts (see earlier today) and let the facts influence our thoughts.

Don't blame; reframe

In a difficult conversation, it's relatively easy to blame the other person: 'It's all your fault that the report is three days late'; 'You should have finished it earlier.' A better way is to see what each side has contributed to the difficulty. Maybe you were slightly late in giving your colleague the figures they needed for the report. Here, it is important to be professional and assert that your aim is not to blame anyone. Instead, you want to discover what went wrong, the reasons for that and what can be done to learn from it.

Turning a difficulty into a learning point

John was in charge of a project to deliver 5,000 books to an exhibition in Germany in October. The text was delivered to the printers on schedule in July but was delayed because one colleague, Douglas, had not filled in the delivery forms correctly. This meant that the books would not reach Germany until November. A decision was therefore made to send the books by air freight to meet the October deadline. The result was a satisfied customer:

the company delivered what they said they would. They focused on fulfilling the customer's expectations, even though they incurred higher costs of air freight.

At an evaluation meeting later, Douglas' manager, Sheila, acted professionally and said she was keen not to blame any one individual. (She had in fact had a quiet, tactful word with Douglas and discovered that his father had died a few days earlier and also that he needed more on-the-job training to develop his role.)

Sheila was careful to avoid public criticism of Douglas but gently probed members of the team: 'How did the situation arise?' 'How did the delay come about?' She was keen to concentrate on the future – what lessons were learned and how internal procedures and communication could be improved. By not focusing on one individual, but by being positive and thinking particularly about what the team could learn for the future, Sheila turned the difficulty into a constructive learning point for the team's development.

Reframe

Reframing is changing the way someone thinks about something they perceive as difficult and negative into seeing it in a more positive manner.

I first encountered this when I was coaching a colleague who hated interviews. She said she did not cope at all well with one-to-one situations. But she also told me she enjoyed negotiating. She relished the challenge of preparing for a negotiation, listening for clues as to the other party's intentions, discussing alternatives and reaching an agreement. So my suggestion that she should reframe her thinking and see interviews positively and as a means of negotiation was a moment of sudden enlightenment for her.

We can reframe a common assumption that someone is untidy: they see themselves as creative. Or someone who is very quiet in meetings: they see themselves as thinking things through before speaking.

Applying this to a difficult conversation, if someone is being excessively critical about minor matters, the way to proceed is not to tell them to stop being like that. Instead you can reframe in a factual way and encourage them to change their perspective by considering neutrally the overall aims of your company and gently ask questions in a positive way. In the case study above, Sheila, the manager, reframed the situation from one in which she could have blamed Douglas and turned it into a positive one – seeing how the situation had developed and how everyone could work together for the good of the company.

Summary

Today we've seen that we cannot ignore emotions in a difficult conversation. Allowing someone to express their own emotions can be an important step in resolving an issue. You may need to explore your own emotional make-up and consider how emotional you are.

One significant step is for a colleague to express and articulate their intentions; this may challenge any assumptions you may have.

We have also seen that the way ahead is not to blame people, criticizing them openly. If we do that, they feel threatened and become defensive. They perceive that their sense of identity is attacked. Rather, it is far better to put resources into affirming colleagues. Reframe the issue and look at the matter in a positive, constructive way.

SUNDAY

MONDAY

TUESDAY

WEDNESDAY

THURSDAY

FRIDAY

SATURDAY

Follow-up

1 How much do you ignore emotions when considering a difficult conversation?

2 How would you describe your own emotional make-up?

3 Do you allow your thoughts to control your emotions or vice versa? Think of times when you have allowed your emotions to control your thoughts. With hindsight, how would you act differently now?

Questions

1. In a difficult conversation, the part played by emotions is:
   a) small ❑
   b) significant ❑
   c) not worth bothering with ❑
   d) the only important matter. ❑

2. Knowing your own emotional make-up is:
   a) useful ❑
   b) a waste of time ❑
   c) 'Shut up!' ❑
   d) the only thing that counts. ❑

3. The way to manage your feelings is to:
   a) emphasize them ❑
   b) eat more bran ❑
   c) manage your thoughts ❑
   d) ignore them. ❑

4. Discussing feelings:
   a) is a waste of time ❑
   b) is important ❑
   c) could become unpleasant so I avoid it ❑
   d) can be helpful if you have the time. ❑

5. I challenge assumptions about other people's intentions:
   a) never ❑
   b) always, so that's all that I do ❑
   c) often ❑
   d) what's an assumption? ❑

6. If someone is expressing their feelings, you should:
   a) interrupt them ❑
   b) tell them to stop and calm down ❑
   c) avoid them ❑
   d) let them do so. ❑

7. After someone has openly expressed their emotions it is important to:
   a) acknowledge such expression as a further step ❑
   b) forget that it ever happened ❑
   c) ignore them for the rest of their career in the company ❑
   d) constantly remind them about the day they cried. ❑

8. When we are criticized:
   a) we feel happy ❑
   b) our sense of identity is affirmed ❑
   c) our sense of identity is upheld ❑
   d) our sense of identity is attacked. ❑

9. If something goes wrong, I want to:
   a) blame the colleague who failed ❑
   b) learn from that mistake ❑
   c) punish the colleague who failed ❑
   d) ignore the whole thing. ❑

10. Reframing is:
    a) seeing something negative from a positive perspective ❑
    b) seeing something positive from a negative perspective ❑
    c) what you do to old photographs ❑
    d) introducing change management. ❑

TUESDAY

Prepare well

Introduction

The focus of this chapter is that careful planning will make your difficult conversation easier. You are probably aware of that and may have learned the hard way, either by initiating a conversation without proper planning or by having been on the receiving end of a conversation that was not planned. Either way, you will have experienced difficulties. So learn from your mistakes as far as you can and determine to plan and organize better.

Specifically, you can plan:

- the venue
- your timing of the conversation
- your opening words
- how you will keep track of the conversation
- how you will end the conversation.

This means that it is unacceptable to arrive at a meeting for a difficult conversation without having prepared for it adequately. If you do not prepare for a difficult conversation, not only do you run the risk of making matters worse, but also you waste valuable time in bringing matters to a successful resolution. Note also that your preparation will increase your confidence and you will feel calmer and more controlled, because you will know the direction your conversation will be taking.

Prepare the venue

The room and seating arrangement in which you conduct your conversation are important. You may not be able to change these, but if you can, there are tips to follow that could help you ease the conversation.

It can be helpful to meet at a neutral venue or in your colleague's office (i.e. not in your office), as you can then leave more easily at an appropriate time.

You have probably been in a room sitting opposite your boss, separated by a big desk. How did you feel? It is better to sit at right angles to a colleague. The atmosphere of the room is also important to encourage people to feel relaxed and in a safe place for them to talk openly. Shut the door to keep noise to a minimum and also sit in such a position that you will not be likely to look around you regularly.

Notice that all this assumes a face-to-face meeting, which is much better than an email 'conversation' or a phone call. It also assumes a private meeting, not a public one, when you may be tempted to criticize a colleague openly in front of their peers.

All participants in the conversation should be seated on chairs at the same level. The room should not be too hot or too cold. It can be helpful to have glasses of water available.

Timing

When possible, tackle the matter sooner rather than later. A small incident can develop into a much more significant pattern if left too long. If possible, give your colleague advance notice that you want to meet with them. 'I'd like to talk to you about ... Can we arrange a time to do this tomorrow?' Giving your colleague advance notice provides them with the opportunity to think about the meeting and what they can say.

If it is not possible to give your colleague notice, then ask them if your suggested time is suitable. If it is not, then plan to meet at a time that is more convenient to you both.

If possible, arrange a meeting for a time when you are not likely to be stressed or tired.

Prepare what you will say

It is important to prepare what you are going to say and plan in advance as much as you can.

● Especially prepare the words that you will begin with: your opening words. These are likely to remain in your colleague's mind. 'I want to talk to you (not 'have a few words with you' which could be thought to mean you want to start an argument). 'There seems to be a discrepancy between the figures that were recorded and the actual figures. I wonder if

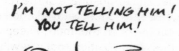

you could comment on that'. ('Seems to be', 'I wonder', 'could' all help ease in the conversation; 'These figures are wrong' is too blunt.) Similarly, telling someone 'You are working too slowly' is too directly provocative, but 'I wonder if you could talk me through the different stages of your work?' is less blunt as an opening statement. And instead of criticizing someone for being incompetent at their job, remind them of the standards they need to fulfil to do a good job.

● For more on this in the context of dealing with specific kinds of colleagues, see Friday.

- Where possible, use positive words. Remember you do not want to provoke an argument.
- Try to keep what you say brief and to the point:

TIP *Prepare your opening words, as these will remain in your colleague's mind.*

- It can be helpful to write down notes for yourself on what you see as the central issue. This will stop you from being easily distracted. If you find that the discussion is wandering away from the core issue, you will find it easier to steer the conversation back on track if you have written down the central issue.
- You might even find it useful to list the points that you do not want to discuss because they are unimportant compared with the central issue. For example, if you are dealing with a boss who keeps on giving you more and more work, it would be unwise to raise matters such as booking a holiday, as that is irrelevant to the main issue.
- Don't only prepare the comments that begin your conversation. Think of the possible ways that your colleague might react and consider in advance how you might respond to each reaction. (In the actual conversation, you might not fully remember your actual plan – it may not be possible to look down at your notes – but any forward thinking and planning you can do is helpful.)
- It is useful to note the effect that your colleague's action has had on you, your work, other colleagues and the wider company or organization. (Look back at the e2c2 model – evidence; effect; change; continue – that was mentioned on Sunday.)
- It could also be helpful to write down feelings that the other person's actions have evoked in you. Such feelings might be of anger, confusion or disappointment.
- Take a lead. As a very junior colleague, and not wanting to take responsibility for leading, I was once so slow at actually starting a conversation that we ran out of time at the end to pursue matters sufficiently thoroughly. Take the initiative, even if you don't feel like doing so; this is your role as manager. If necessary, push yourself to do this.

Being positive

Rebecca wasn't getting on with her colleague Sally. Sally had been promoted and Rebecca felt insecure about this, but they still had to work together. They realized that they disagreed with each other, but rather than focusing on what they did not like about each other, they concentrated on discussing their strengths and what a good working relationship would look like between them. They identified that Rebecca was better at thinking through the detailed consequences of decisions than Sally, who often tended to communicate her ideas without having thought them through. They decided to sit down before the next important meeting to share their strengths. By committing to work together and being positive, they learned to collaborate effectively.

Use 'I', not 'you' statements

Statements such as 'You're always late' or 'You're so inconsiderate' are unhelpful. Instead, rephrase the point you're trying to make as an 'I' statement: 'I feel ... when you ... because ...'. The result is, for example, 'I feel disappointed when you're late with the work because we need to get the financial reports out from our department on time. The result of your being late is that colleagues in other departments waste time by sitting around doing nothing. Or they have to base their figures on previous months' data which do not give an accurate picture of our financial position.'

Here we come back to Sunday's e2c2 model: you are expressing the effect that your colleague's work has. Further, mentioning your own feelings lessens the defensiveness of your colleague. In contrast, if you had said, 'You're always late' they may have felt personally threatened and defensive. Finally, using an 'I' statement shows the reasons why you want to talk about the issue. By raising these wider aspects, your colleague may well see the further effects of their actions and so may feel more inclined to talk about and tackle the issue.

Being clear so that you are not misinterpreted

Sophie remembers being a new manager when she had to take her first junior colleague through the company's disciplinary capability procedure. Sophie had the initial informal meeting with Jack, in which she explained her concerns, gave him certain objectives and described the support she would put in place to help him achieve them. This was followed up with a written record of the meeting. They then came to review it a month later. Sophie had to give Jack everything she was going to raise with him in the meeting beforehand. He came to the meeting with his union representative, saying that he was unaware that he was part of a disciplinary process, and thought the last meeting was about preparing him for promotion!

Sophie had to learn not to be too cautious and unsure. Her message was unclear and ambiguous so Jack had missed the point. Sophie had wanted to soften the blow, and somehow Jack had misinterpreted the nature of the meeting. What Sophie should have done was to get Jack to say back to her what she had said so that she could have checked his understanding and made sure he had grasped what was happening. (Of course, it could have been a tactic to prolong the procedure, because they had to repeat the first informal stage again ... in fact, Jack resigned at the end of the following month.)

Be factual where possible and clearly mention specific matters: 'The report is due every Thursday at 12p.m. Over the last three weeks you've delivered it on Friday at 10a.m., Friday at 11a.m. and Thursday at 5p.m.' However, avoid such words as 'always' and 'never'. They tend to be inaccurate and can arouse feelings of hostility. Stay calm.

Check your colleague has understood what you have said

When you make comments to your colleague, you want to know that they have accurately received your communication.

Sometimes you can tell that they have understood what you are saying from how the conversation proceeds; at other times you may need to ask explicitly: 'Have I explained this clearly enough or are you more confused?' Their response will help you decide what you should say next, adjusting it to their particular response.

For more on summarizing at the end of a conversation, see Friday.

Keep the conversation focused

Your role is to keep the conversation going as far as you can. Have a specific aim in mind for each particular conversation. Realize that this conversation may be part of a series, so your goal may be simply to move on a stage and then to allow your colleague time and opportunity to reflect before a further meeting to resume the conversation. For example, if you want your colleague to take on further responsibility, your first meeting might be to raise the matter with them in principle – and also to begin to think about areas they could delegate to others. Then at a later meeting you could agree the details of when they could actually start the new work.

ALL RIGHT, THEN — LET'S HAVE A DISCUSSION ABOUT WHETHER TO HAVE A DISCUSSION

So the rule is: don't allow the conversation to be sidetracked. Make sure you do not become taken up with a subject that is different from the main one you want to pursue. If you go into a meeting with only a vague aim, you will achieve that – vagueness – but if your aim is clear in your own mind, then you are far more likely to achieve what you want. Make sure the conversation is progressing in a way that fits in with your goal.

Take a break

If meetings take place over a few weeks, then the time between meetings allows opportunity for reflection and to prepare yourself again.

If the meetings are at shorter intervals, for example they take place in the same day, you can introduce a break for a short while – even 10 or 15 minutes can enable both sides to take a rest before needing to concentrate their thoughts again. Sometimes new thoughts occur when you are not thinking about the issue: your subconscious mind is given the opportunity to do its work and fresh ideas can emerge.

Offer suggestions

In your preparation for a difficult conversation:

● Consider the interests – motives, concerns and needs – of both 'sides': yours and those of your colleague. Remember, the more fully you understand your colleague's interests, the more successful your discussion is likely to be.
● Consider several possible creative ways of moving towards resolving the issue and the advantages such solutions would bring. Focus initially on your colleague's strengths (good points), main interests and priorities. Your aim is to move on from simply discussing the same points; you want to resolve the issue. For example, if a colleague is underperforming then you, as manager, could suggest that the colleague should email you a list of the work that they have completed at the end of every day. In this way, by keeping a close track of what they are doing, you can monitor their work and see if they need to make further adjustments to the overall work flow going through their department.

Your suggestions are just that: suggestions, but they are also a basis for objective evaluation, negotiation and discussion. For example, 'I would rather delay the introduction of the new computer system for three months until after Christmas, so that it doesn't interfere with our Christmas orders. What do you think?' Or to help a colleague look at the consequences of their actions, you could ask them, 'Is this what you want to happen?' If the answer is 'No' then you could explore with them the different options to change that outcome.

> **TIP** *Consider creative ways of resolving the issue and the advantages each solution would bring.*

End well

Ensure that outcomes are clearly agreed. You may want to make sure that the goals are SMART:

- **S** Specific, defining the desired results, not vague
- **M** Measurable and quantifiable, so that you know whether the objectives have been reached (e.g. with milestones along the way to assess progress)
- **A** Agreed by all present at the meeting
- **R** Realistic: objectives that are achievable: not too easy but those that will develop and challenge ('stretch') the colleague's resources and skills
- **T** Timed: when are the actions to be completed by?

Some colleagues also add –ER to give SMARTER:

- **E** Evaluated: at a later meeting, progress is assessed
- **R** Reported: the evaluation is recorded at a future meeting.

If necessary, confirm the outcomes in writing with your colleague. It is important that your colleague knows what their responsibility is. You may also want to discuss and agree how they are to do it. Be clear. If you are giving someone responsibility to lead a project, be clear about the upper limit of money they can spend without seeking further authorization from you.

You may agree to meet on a certain date to review progress, to ensure overall objectives are met and to check that any obstacles have been overcome.

Finally, ask your colleague to summarize again precisely what they have agreed to do and the date(s) by which they have agreed to undertake it. Their repetition of this aspect will help seal it in their minds and you can address any gaps or misunderstandings sooner rather than later.

A well-prepared appraisal

Manfred had worked for the organization for 25 years, was a department head, and had been co-opted from his usual responsibilities to work with a different team managed by its own department head. Owen, a subordinate manager within that team, had worked for the organization for 12 months, having been recruited from an organization of similar business but quite different culture.

In general Owen had settled in well, but tended not to move away from 'that's how we did it in Xxx' and did not always recognize the different culture of his new organization.

Some of Manfred's skills differed from the team's specialisms, but many were complementary. The team worked collectively and also in pairs, and regularly Owen and Manfred would be paired. Their relationship was difficult, principally because Owen considered that in the team's day-to-day activities his own experience was superior to Manfred's, and although Manfred never disputed this, he was less happy working with Owen than when working with others whose skills he shared and with whom he enjoyed greater affinity.

Manfred was not Owen's line manager, but he was asked to write and deliver Owen's annual appraisal. There were good points of Owen's work to discuss, but there were also issues to explore requiring change for the future, many of them culture related, and these were likely to be problematic. Manfred felt it was quite possible that Owen's disregard for their working relationship could get in the way of objective discussion about other issues, a potential case of 'shooting the messenger'.

Before the appraisal, Manfred pondered the approach he should take. Rather than address the change issues as behavioural or personal, he decided to deal with them from the perspective of them being a by-product of the organization itself not having addressed the likelihood of them occurring, and failing to put in place appropriate structures to forestall such issues.

By starting off positively, and then introducing the issues for remedy on the basis of what the organization needed to do to bring about the required change, Manfred managed to head off any personal thoughts Owen might have harboured regarding his doubt of Manfred's ability to deliver his appraisal. This approach gave the discussion an objective focus. For instance, not having provided an all-round induction and not having given Owen greater knowledge of the organization or exposure to the wider business had restricted his focus to the immediate area of his own working. The solution was for the organization to improve the induction training and insight given to new entrants, and for Owen to work on increasing his awareness of the organization beyond the confines of his immediate surroundings.

Owen readily accepted the issues as presented, seeing them as his personal responsibility to the organization and quite separate from his working relationship with Manfred.

Ultimately both sides felt that the appraisal had been a worthwhile and positive exercise, resulting in a clear and agreed plan for the future.

By preparing well – recognizing how the meeting was likely to proceed, thinking about the ultimate objectives of the appraisal, and planning a strategy to forestall any divergence from the task in hand – the appraisal maintained objectivity and was successful.

Summary

Today we've been concerned with preparing and planning. If you fail to prepare, you are preparing to fail. A well-prepared conversation is far more likely to go well than one that you have not prepared for.

You will have prepared the room in which you will hold the conversation and the most convenient time in which to hold it.

You will have planned your opening and how you will proceed in a positive way, focusing on reaching your goal.

You will have worked through your colleague's possible responses and how you will react to them, keeping the conversation on track to reach the desired conclusion.

Follow-up

Think of a difficult conversation
you need to have:

1 What can you do to prepare for it?

2 Where would be the best place to hold it?
When would be the best time to hold it?

3 What do you see as the main issue?

4 How you will begin? What exact words
will you use?

5 How might your colleague respond? What
will you do to deal with their responses?

6 What is your aim for the conversation?
How might you be sidetracked?

Questions

1. The best way to conduct a difficult conversation is:
a) by email ❑
b) on the phone ❑
c) in text messages ❑
d) in a face-to-face meeting. ❑

2. Spending time thinking about the timing of the difficult conversation and the arrangement of the room is:
a) wasted ❑
b) unimportant ❑
c) essential ❑
d) useful. ❑

3. Preparing your opening words is:
a) vital ❑
b) unimportant – I will say the first thing that comes into my mind ❑
c) a waste of time ❑
d) useful if I remember to do it. ❑

4. In a difficult conversation, it is important to:
a) be as negative as possible, so they know how you feel ❑
b) be as unclear as possible, to waste time ❑
c) be as positive as possible, to help your colleague ❑
d) be as direct as possible, to embarrass your colleague. ❑

5. In a difficult conversation, it is important to:
a) not discuss anything that might introduce change ❑
b) avoid the main issue as it is too painful to discuss ❑
c) be clear about the central issue ❑
d) become sidetracked to keep the conversation going. ❑

6. It is better to use:
a) unclear statements ❑
b) 'I' rather than 'you' statements ❑
c) 'you' rather than 'I' statements ❑
d) words such as 'always' and 'never'. ❑

7. It is important to be:
a) clear and factual ❑
b) subjective ❑
c) critical ❑
d) vague. ❑

8. When the discussion becomes sidetracked:
a) I am happy, because you can think about something else ❑
b) I bring it back to the main issue ❑
c) I don't know what the main issue is in the first place ❑
d) I let the conversation become even more sidetracked. ❑

9. In your preparation, you should also think of:
a) ways of going home early ☐
b) direct responses to resolve the issue proactively ☐
c) distractions to avoid resolving the main issue ☐
d) creative suggestions to move the discussion forward to resolve the issue. ☐

10. At the end of the difficult conversation, you should:
a) start arguing again ☐
b) confirm the actions with your colleague ☐
c) ask your colleague to confirm what they will do ☐
d) don't bother summarizing; just go home. ☐

WEDNESDAY

Listen carefully

Introduction

Have you ever jumped to conclusions about a person without knowing all the facts? What happened? Most of us have had to learn the hard way to listen first, before drawing conclusions. Today is all about listening ... listening until you discern the real issues.

When thinking about difficult conversations we tend immediately to think of our responsibility in speaking. We want to say the most appropriate words. But alongside that, we need to remember that our speaking is not isolated from its context. We speak in certain situations, and listening carefully has to come before speaking to enable what we say to be effective.

So today we consider:

- the importance of listening
- how to listen more attentively, focusing on what the other person is saying
- steps to help us listen more effectively.

We then consider the art of asking incisive questions that get to the heart of an issue, the root problem of a difficult conversation.

Listen more attentively

The comments today focus on listening in face-to-face relationships. As a manager, you will be expected to do a lot of listening not only in difficult conversations with colleagues but also to your boss as they direct your work, to colleagues as you talk about your work and in meetings as you discuss a range of subjects and make decisions.

Listening is hard work

How can you listen more attentively in the work situation? You are already working hard at being a manager. Part of your hard work – not additional to it – is listening. Listening will enable you to manage and encourage members of your team more effectively. As you improve your listening skills, you will learn again that listening is important and you will gain a deeper understanding of your colleagues. But note that listening is not an end in itself; it is a means to an end. Listening enables you to ask incisive questions, ones that help you explore deeper issues.

There are many reasons why listening is difficult:

- We tend to focus on what we want to say in pursuing our own priorities, which may be to quickly advise or persuade a colleague to follow a certain path. By contrast, listening demands that our concentration is on someone else as we follow the sequence of their thoughts.
- The person we're listening to may speak unclearly, too fast or repeat themselves.
- The person we're listening to may be a non-native speaker and so does not speak in standard English.
- We were probably not taught to listen. I vaguely remember school lessons trying to teach us the other language skills of reading, writing and speaking but I don't think I was ever taught to listen (or maybe I wasn't listening during those lessons!).

But listening is a really valuable skill. Have you ever felt really burdened by something and opened your heart to someone else? At the end you feel relieved and can say, 'Thank you for listening.'

 TIP *Listening is far more than merely hearing.*

The importance of listening

Listening:

- focuses on the other person. Often when someone else is talking, we're focusing on thinking about what we are going to say as a reply.
- values the person you are listening to as an individual in their own right, so that you understand someone better, why they are working or speaking as they do. So listening helps you understand the point at which a person is.
- encourages you to ask the right questions. As you focus on the other person (not yourself), you will want to know more. We can distinguish:
  - closed questions: ones that can be answered by a straight 'Yes' or 'No': 'Was the project late?' 'Yes.' 'Will you be able to give me the figures by 5p.m.?' 'No.'

- open questions: ones that get people talking. Open questions begin with *why, how, who, when, where, what*. 'Why do you think the project is running late?' 'Because we didn't plan enough time for the extra work the customer now wants.' Most of the questions you should ask as a manager should be open questions, to explore the other person's perceptions and experiences.

● means that you do not listen only to the words a colleague is speaking: you can perceive their response to what you are saying by being sensitive to their body language and tone of voice.

● allows you to 'listen between the lines', to become aware of any underlying messages, such as that they are unhappy about being undervalued at work.

● allows you to distinguish between facts and opinions. You will hear both, and you can discern what is objective information and what are the subjective thoughts on such information. You are then in a position to evaluate what has been said.

● enables you to gather information so that you can solve problems, make decisions more efficiently and move a difficult conversation forward.

● builds trust between people: you show that you are genuinely interested in them. This forms the basis to help you work well with them. Listening often improves relationships. Rather than someone keeping angry feelings to themselves and becoming increasingly tense, listening – and allowing someone to speak openly about their difficulties – provides a release for them.

● offers an opportunity to develop more all-round relationships. For example if a colleague says, 'I'm off on holiday tomorrow,' you can either ignore that signal (but ignoring it is possibly slightly rude) or you can use that as a hint that they want to tell you more about themselves: 'Great, where are you going?' 'Hong Kong'. You can then remember to ask them 'How was Hong Kong?' when you next see them.

● can resolve disagreements. If colleagues are in conflict with one another, listening to and understanding the opinions of the other side – not necessarily agreeing with them – is an important step in settling a disagreement.

● helps you understand people better. As you listen carefully to someone, you will discover more about that person: what is important to them, how they think and what they are feeling. Recently a stressed-out colleague told me, 'I want to go back to Australia.' That seemed to tell me a lot about her: a desire to be released from present tensions and return to a former, more relaxed environment. Having such knowledge helps you work better with them, even if you don't like them or agree with their opinions.

Susie was angry

Susie was angry. She worked late every evening to complete her tasks in the project but she felt her work was not appreciated or valued. It was only when a new colleague, Jan, started to work alongside her that something happened. Jan was concerned less about herself and her own work (which she did well) and more about her colleague – she cared enough to stop and listen to Susie. Susie was in tears as she poured out her heart to Jan, telling her about the real pressures she was working under. At the end of their conversation Susie told Jan, 'Thanks for listening. You're the first person I've been able to talk to about these things.'

Tips on better listening

Here are some ways to help you improve your listening skills:

● Be curious. Suppose a colleague has just completed an exam and you ask her how it went and she replies, 'I answered most of the questions OK.' What she is probably hoping is that you will be curious and ask about the questions that she was not happy with. She has used the word 'most' in the hope that you will respond to that. So you need to be alert to go beyond the surface – the words someone uses – and watch for the feelings that are expressed. So you could say, 'When you said you answered most of the questions OK, did you find some of them hard?' and she will probably open up and talk about the questions that she found difficult. Such curiosity should be a gentle probing conducted in a way that will not be perceived as aggressive or as part of an interrogation. You are not cross-examining your colleague as if they were a witness in a law court!

● Be responsible. Realize that listening is an active skill and as such is hard work. Concentrate. For example, when I meet someone for the first time, I listen particularly attentively to catch their name. If I think I've heard it accurately, I'll say it back to them, 'Great to meet you Nick!' If I didn't hear their name properly, I'll say, 'I'm sorry I didn't quite catch your name' or ask (if it is unusual to me and seems difficult to spell) 'Could you spell that for me please?'

TIP *Don't be tempted to interrupt the other person while they are talking.*

● Focus on the other person, not yourself. Stop and really listen to what the other person is saying. Make eye contact with them. Be interested in them. Rephrase what they've said in your own way to help you clarify the meaning in your own mind, and express that. For example, 'So what you're really saying is that we should have put in place more effective monitoring controls.' 'So the way you see it is ...' Such a rephrasing process is called 'reflective listening'. This shows that you've heard the heart (both the actual words and any underlying emotions) of what your colleague was trying to express. You do not have to agree with what the other person says; that is not the point. Your reflective listening shows that you take them seriously.

● Be sincere. We say 'How are you?' so many times a day without really wanting to know how someone is feeling. Sometimes, if trusted friends ask me 'How are you?' and I am having a difficult day I will answer, 'Do you really want to know?' That takes them aback and if they sincerely answer

'Yes' (as they usually do), I will unburden myself a little. People can tell when colleagues are practising a technique or are being genuine and sincere.

- Be willing to accept the reasoning and opinions of others as valid. Be willing to acknowledge that you may have made false assumptions and may have prejudices.
- Discern the main points of what is being said. Speakers may or may not structure their argument well. Often, in informal talks or meetings, it can be difficult to distinguish between facts, opinions, examples and ideas, but try to work out the speaker's main point(s). Ask further questions or make further statements to clarify so that you understand your colleague's thoughts. Examples are: 'I wonder if you could give me an example of ...?' 'Have I got this right ...?' 'So are you saying ...?' 'It sounds as though ...'.
- Do your best to remain attentive, even if the other person is not; do not become distracted.
- Write down in note form what a speaker is saying if you might otherwise forget it and need to remember. Making notes can help you concentrate and avoid the sense that 'things go in one ear and out of the other'.
- Don't interrupt the person who is speaking. Your role is to wait patiently and listen attentively: this may be difficult when time is short, you want to resolve the issue quickly or you have a different opinion from the person you are listening to. If, however, you do stop yourself from interrupting and listen patiently, you may well get to the basic source of the difficulty.
- Don't be afraid of silence; learn to be comfortable with it. Silence is part of a conversation. It can be:
  - a junction: which way will a conversation turn?
  - a time to catch up and digest what has been said
  - an opportunity for the other person to express their thoughts further
  - an opportunity to reflect on what has been said.
- Be aware of your body language, especially if you are nervous. Avoid body language that could be perceived as being negative. So don't fold your arms (in boredom) or look

around you (in distraction). Instead encourage your colleague to go on talking and show your genuine interest by:
- leaning forward slightly
- expressing a responsive reaction in your face
- nodding occasionally as a response of understanding what your colleague is saying
- speaking in a calm, warm, interested and sensitive tone of voice
- uttering such brief verbal cues as 'I see' or 'mmm'.

Listening helps you gain a deeper understanding

Have you ever stepped in and tried to resolve an issue only to find out that you are missing a vital piece of information? Because you stepped in too early, you did not know the full picture. You acted too hastily and jumped to the wrong conclusions.

Don't jump to conclusions

During one of the frequent end-of-year travel restrictions, John had a call from Bill, his fair but humourless boss who was his Regional Manager. Bill angrily informed John that he had just returned from a conference in Berlin, dutifully obeying the 'Economy Class only' rule that he himself had instigated, only to see Fiona, one of John's team, happily settling into row 3 of the plane in Business Class. 'This is the last straw! Sack that woman!' Bill instructed John before hanging up.

That was John's first difficult conversation, but he was now facing an even more difficult one with Fiona. While she was an independent, somewhat unconventional, person, she was a well-liked member of the team and greatly respected by customers. John certainly didn't want to lose her from the company.

John and Fiona had a meeting to establish why she had done it and what they needed to do next. After the

meeting, John reflected how it had gone, and he realized
he had learned a number of valuable lessons in handling
confrontational situations:

● Do not to take things at face value. It turned out that
Fiona was using a ticket from a previously cancelled trip;
in fact the flight had not cost the company anything.
Understandably she had not asked for a downgrade to
Economy Class!

● Do not to move too quickly to reach a conclusion. While
'sacking' had never been an option, John had intended to
reprimand Fiona, which in the circumstances would have
been seen by her as a huge injustice.

● Do make sure everyone understands the real issues.
This was not about class of travel; it was about the humili-
ation of the boss and the injustice he felt. Fiona and John
discussed this and John asked her how she would have
felt if the positions had been reversed.

● Do ensure justice is seen to be done. Both Bill and Fiona had to feel that their points had been heard. She had
the satisfaction of explaining the situation and appearing
blameless, and John could inform Bill that there had been
a 'serious conversation' about the incident.

● Finally, never expect thanks! Both parties would end
up feeling slightly aggrieved, but John had managed to
placate an angry manager and the company retained
a loyal and successful employee. John felt it was a job
well done.

Ask incisive questions

Incisive questions show that you are able to think clearly about
something, that you have both a good understanding of what is
significant and also the ability to express such understanding.
Incisive questions can move the conversation forward. The
focus isn't so much on 'What should I say?' but 'What should
I ask?' Such questions will show that you have the ability to
notice and understand things that are not obvious – that you

can judge people and situations intelligently and accurately. An incisive question may challenge an assumption and get to the heart of an issue.

As we saw earlier today, we can distinguish between closed questions that can be answered by a straight 'Yes' or 'No' ('Was the project late?' 'Yes.') and open questions, which encourage people to talk more and share their perceptions and experiences. Open questions begin with *why, how, who, when, where, what*: 'What is stopping you from coming to work on time?' 'Why do you think the project ran late?' Such questions put the responsibility back on the other person rather than allowing them to evade the responsibility.

Repeating the example above, if you ask your colleague 'When you said you answered most of the questions OK, did you find some of them hard?' they will probably open up and talk about those hard questions. I sometimes ask 'How do you feel about ...?' because colleagues are not often asked that; instead they are more often asked more concrete questions, such as 'When will you do this by?' and directly asking them about their feelings gives them an opportunity to open up.

Listening will give you certain information from what a person says. It may also show you things from what a person does not say. I talked with a colleague over several years and knew her quite well, but I noticed she often mentioned her mother, but never her father, so one day I asked about her father.

So if a person is late with a piece of work, rather than saying, 'Why are you late with it?' or 'You didn't do that very well, did you?' you could probe, 'What kinds of things are you finding difficult in the work?' or be more specific and focused: 'How can we help you meet the deadline for next month's report?'

Questions should be to the point and relevant to the issue being discussed. For example, you could ask, 'I'd like to hear your thoughts on ...'

It is usually not appropriate to ask personal questions about a relationship with a partner. Good questions are focused on the issue being discussed and will move the conversation forward so that the issue is closer to being resolved.

As you ask incisive and probing questions, you can reveal something of your motives for doing so, i.e. give your colleague the bigger picture. If you do not do this, your questions could seem to be threatening and make the person you are talking to defensive. But if you share your reasons – 'I'm asking because I really want to know how you think we reached this situation.' 'I'd like to find out more about how you feel about the new systems we've introduced because ...' – things may become easier in the long term.

Deeper issues

If we are dealing with a colleague and an issue, sometimes there is a deeper underlying issue. It seems as if the colleague we are discussing an issue with is testing us out, to see whether they can trust us as they open up to us on a relatively unimportant area of life. If we respond sensitively to begin with, then that colleague may entrust us with the real issue, but often we are not aware of that and solve only the less important problem.

I heard of a teacher who said that, when talking with parents about their child's special education needs, the parents can sometimes not be ready to hear the truth.

They expect to have a normal, happy and healthy child. They are being faced with the fact that their child is not that child. They almost have to grieve for the child they have lost, before they can accept the child they have. It can be the same receiving any message you try to deliver in a difficult conversation: a person won't hear if they don't want to or they're not in a place to receive it.

Perceptive listening

Max was an outside consultant and he arrived early at Peterson's Ltd where he was due to lead a one-day course on team communication skills. Sarah asked if he wanted a cup of coffee and Max accepted. Immediately, Jim, a colleague of Sarah's suddenly spoke up in an unexpectedly angry tone. 'You never make me a cup of coffee.' At once, Max sensed tension between the two colleagues. Max soon discovered that all the colleagues in the company were on one of two opposing sides, but over the course of the day he successfully managed to get the two sides to talk to each other. Later on, he discovered the root problem for the lack of communication. Jim felt he had been unfairly treated when he had been passed over to be project team leader and the job had been given to Sarah, who was younger than Jim and whom Jim considered to be far less experienced than him. Over time, two groups had developed, each supporting an opposing faction. Fortunately, Max was able to begin to help them overcome their differences and work together to complete the project.

By listening perceptively, being sensitive to people and the relationships between them and probing gently, Max was able to move the team on in a significant way.

'But we have to talk at some point'

At first Sam didn't know what he could do when Carole wouldn't communicate. Carole just sat there in sullen silence, refusing to say anything. Sam realized that her so-called 'lack of communication' did in fact communicate a lot, for example that Carole felt threatened by the whole situation. Sam knew it wasn't helpful to keep asking Carole, 'What's the matter?' or 'What's wrong?' Instead, Sam respected Carole's right to remain silent at that time so said, 'Carole, you don't have to say anything now. But we have to talk at some point.' By allowing Carole time to reflect, Sam was giving her the power – and the responsibility – to resume the conversation when Carole felt it was safe to do so.

Summary

Today we've considered listening skills and the ability to ask incisive questions. Listening is hard work ... but rewarding.

Follow-up

1 Ask colleagues if they think you are a good listener or not. *Listen* to their response.

2 Think about a recent business conversation. Were you too busy thinking about what you wanted to say that you did not really listen to the person you were talking to?

3 What do you need to stop doing in order to listen more effectively?

4 What positive steps can you take to improve your listening skills? Ask your colleagues to help you.

5 How often do you tend to jump to conclusions, without letting a colleague talk further so that you get to the basic issue?

6 What practical steps can you take to ask more incisive questions? When will you next have the opportunity to do this?

Questions

1. The key skill in listening is:
   a) looking at a person's face ❑
   b) thinking about what you want to say ❑
   c) focusing on what the other person is saying ❑
   d) looking at the floor. ❑

2. Good listening:
   a) develops worse relationships ❑
   b) provokes arguments ❑
   c) relaxes people ❑
   d) develops better working relationships. ❑

3. Listening is:
   a) easy – that's why I'm the manager ❑
   b) hard work, but rewarding ❑
   c) not worth bothering about ❑
   d) useful if I have the time. ❑

4. When I listen well, I:
   a) can discern the main points someone is trying to communicate ❑
   b) am confused ❑
   c) get easily distracted ❑
   d) interrupt the other person. ❑

5. Listening provides a basis for me to:
   a) express my own opinion to anyone who will listen ❑
   b) ask further questions ❑
   c) decide what to eat for lunch ❑
   d) work out who I like and who I don't. ❑

6. Letting people talk without interrupting them:
   a) takes too long and I'm in a hurry ❑
   b) is annoying ❑
   c) is easy as long as I don't need to listen to them ❑
   d) means that I get to the heart of the issue. ❑

7. Asking questions to clarify an issue is:
   a) a waste of time ❑
   b) essential ❑
   c) useful if I have the time ❑
   d) a technique I've never understood. ❑

8. I rephrase what a colleague is saying:
   a) always, so that it annoys them ❑
   b) occasionally, to keep myself awake ❑
   c) never; that would be disrespectful ❑
   d) often, to help clarify what they are saying. ❑

9. My body language in a difficult conversation shows:
   a) that I have learned techniques ❑
   b) that I am bored ❑
   c) that I am sensitive ❑
   d) that I am in a hurry to go home. ❑

10. The questions I ask in a difficult conversation are:

a) aggressive, to make my colleague defensive ☐

b) personal, to embarrass my colleague ☐

c) superficial, not to upset anyone ☐

d) incisive, to get to the root of the problem. ☐

THURSDAY

Treat colleagues with respect

Introduction

What is your aim in a difficult conversation? To move people on, to resolve issues. But the way in which you do this is important. It is all too easy to come across as aggressive or as wanting to assert your power and humiliate your colleague. If you follow that path, you may win the battle but the relationship with your colleague may have become soured.

Today, therefore, we explore treating colleagues with respect by considering:

- affirming your colleague
- continuing to listen to your colleague until they feel heard
- stating your point of view clearly
- remaining courteous, even during the times when you disagree with your colleague
- demonstrating empathy with your colleague, feeling 'into' their situation
- being explicit about your motives
- asserting yourself – this means being neither passive nor aggressive
- saying no at times, and doing this graciously.

Affirm others

Yesterday we looked at listening skills. Putting such skills in the context of what we have been discussing this week, we have seen that listening skills are vital in discovering your colleague's:

- thoughts and feelings about their present position
- needs, such as to be valued
- interests and aims in how they think the situation can be moved on.

But how do you respond to your colleagues as they talk and express themselves? You can show your understanding by saying, 'I see' or responding, 'hmmm.' These express reassurance and are a signal to your colleague to continue to talk. Nodding occasionally helps, but please note that these are suggestions that you could use as a genuine part of your style of communication, not as techniques that you have learned. In other words, be natural, be yourself. Colleagues can discern when you are not being authentic.

As your colleague talks and you respond, you will discover more about them. You may discover that you understand your colleague but that you disagree with them: what do you do then?

The point is clear: your aim is still to respect your colleague as a person, even though you may disagree with them. Remember that your body language and tone of voice can reveal such thoughts. I was at a meeting with other managers and a high-level colleague used a high-pitched tone when mentioning another colleague who had recently been promoted (surprisingly, in the eyes of that high-level colleague). The high pitch revealed her wonder at this promotion.

If you were to express such thoughts out loud, they would be likely to make your colleague angry and possibly hostile towards you. If you were to express such thoughts out loud and then try to withdraw them later by apologizing for making them, your colleague would still think, 'So that's what they really think of me!'

We need to resist the temptation to be drawn downwards into disrespecting one another, even when we don't agree with our colleagues.

Listen until you understand how your colleague really feels.

Continue to listen until your colleague feels heard

We're back to Wednesday's theme again. Listen until you understand how your colleague feels. Don't say, 'I know how you feel' or 'I understand what you are going through.' If you say that, your colleague is unlikely to believe you. As you listen, listen beyond the words to your colleague's feelings. Such feelings are normal. You acknowledge and say that they are valid. Your aim is to truly understand and to communicate your thoughts back to your colleague. Deal with their perceptions. You will discover and identify your colleague's interests, concerns and needs. For me, it takes courage to express my thoughts and to see if I have accurately reflected what my colleague is thinking and feeling. It takes courage because I don't want to be wrong: it is simpler just to nod without really understanding my colleague. But I am learning to rise above such practice and to respond to my colleague to some extent, knowing that I have not fully grasped what my colleague is saying but also knowing that my first attempt is just that – part of the process of understanding my colleague fully. They may then say, 'That's not it.' Or, 'You've not got it quite right' and then elaborate how you were inaccurate. For example, you could say, 'It sounds to me as if the basic issue is that you've committed yourself to their company for years but no one is really valuing your work or expressing their genuine appreciation for your contribution to the team.'

Ultimately you will be in a position where you have discovered the most important issue, which may not have been the issue that your colleague started out with. For example, the original issue might have been a disagreement over a minor problem, but your discussion reveals the more important underlying issue is one of trust: 'You don't trust me as leader of this organization.'

You may then be in a position to identify with your colleague by expressing your observations about your own or others' experience. For example, a colleague was late in completing a very long report. What worked best in helping her complete it was my saying, 'Yes, when I wrote a similar report a few years ago, it seemed like I was always a few days away from completing it.' I had sensed her frustration at genuinely wanting to do a good job but the whole project was taking far longer than she had wanted. My sharing her common feeling and experience increased my credibility with her.

Guy was a good listener

Guy felt low. He'd just been promoted and had been pleased with that ... for a few weeks. Then his boss had resigned and he was suddenly faced with matters that he didn't know how to handle. In particular, he'd had to appraise the performance of a colleague, Petra, and the meeting had started badly. Guy wasn't prepared as he didn't know Petra at all and he hadn't had time to check out her work. Petra felt unappreciated and expressed the view that several different managers were giving her too much work. She had even been sent on a time-management course which had helped a little but the real problem was that her managers were weak and poor communicators who seemed unable to make clear decisions.

But Guy was a good listener and as he listened to Petra, seeking to affirm her, he realized that she had excellent skills of being organized, good with people and also (she let slip) she was good at speaking Portuguese. Guy's sensitivity to Petra's skills enabled him to move her to become PA to the Brazilian sales director, as Brazil was opening up as a new market. Petra flourished in her new role.

State your point of view

After your colleague really feels heard, i.e. when you have discovered the real (or root) cause or issue, you can then express your viewpoint. We discussed on Tuesday the need to choose your words carefully. Be brief, positive and clear. Be courageous and also reveal your feelings about the issue. Remember that the issue is not only the actual issue but also the feelings surrounding the issue. Until the emotional issues are dealt with, the main issue probably cannot be solved.

Be courteous

Sometimes in our desire to deal with an issue effectively, we can forget the small details of polite manners and appropriate behaviour.

- Act and speak politely: shaking someone's hand when you greet them, saying 'please' and 'thank you', 'May I clarify …'
- Avoid expressing yourself in a careless or rash way (see the comments on Tuesday on preparing what you will say). Be professional; don't gossip.

- Be aware of your personality. My personality is (generally!) gentle and I need to push myself to be firmer and more explicitly assertive. If your natural tendency is to be dominant, then at times practise being gentler. My experience is that others will treat you in the same way that you treat them. So if you speak aggressively to someone, they may well respond aggressively to you, whereas if you adopt a calmer, kinder approach, colleagues are more likely to speak back in such a manner too.

- It is easier to begin more calmly and if necessary adopt a firmer approach. If you begin aggressively, not only is your colleague likely to become defensive and respond aggressively, but also it will be difficult to change your approach to a calmer one.
- Remain courteous; remember your aim is not for you to win and for your colleague to lose. Ensure you maintain respect for your colleague; your intention is not to humiliate them or make them look foolish. Don't be sarcastic or patronizing. Discuss issues openly and honestly. Be genuine, sincere and authentic.
- Demonstrate empathy, a feeling 'into' another person's situation. As you listen to your colleague, you discover their interests and motives. For example, you begin to feel their hurt at being undervalued. You identify with them; you have understood what caused their feelings. You also communicate your understanding to them: you help them realize you perceive the situation as they do. This will show others that you genuinely understand them and that you respect them.
- Be explicit about your motives. Because you are determined to rise above petty office politics, you will want to act professionally for the wider benefit of the whole company or organization. For example, if you merely state in a meeting that you think the budget for another department should be lower in the next financial year without giving any reasons to support your statement, then you should not be surprised if you antagonize members of that department. If, on the other hand, you explain your reasons, then colleagues at least have a basis for a discussion.
- Apologize where appropriate. Some books suggest you should never apologize but that seems unreal to me. If you have made a mistake, be genuine and say you are sorry: 'I'm sorry I forgot to tell you the meeting was cancelled.' If you have sincerely expressed your regret at what you did do, or failed to do, then if necessary you can explain the genuine reasons why you forgot and move on to pursue the greater purpose.
- Don't use 'I'm sorry' to reduce the impact of bad news. So, rather than saying, 'I'm sorry we can't give you a pay rise this year', you could genuinely say, 'We really do wish we could

afford to give you a pay rise this year. Here are some of the possibilities, such as giving staff a week's extra holiday ...'

● Express the relevant extent of physical contact, for example to show empathy. The extent of physical contact varies from one culture to another. In most cultures, physical contact is inappropriate:
  – if there is the possibility that it would make the other person feel uncomfortable
  – if it does not fit the social situation or the relationship between the colleagues up to that point.

● Remain professional if your colleague is visibly distressed. If a colleague starts crying during your conversation, you should stop the conversation and ask them if they would like a break, perhaps for a few minutes, before starting again. Show that you understand that this is upsetting for them by saying 'I realize this is disappointing news for you' or something similar.

● At the end, affirm your relationship positively, for example: 'We may not be in complete agreement about all the issues, Freda, but you remain a trusted colleague and I will continue to respect you.'

Introducing changes gradually

Martha was promoted to team leader and had many good ideas on changing things, for example by introducing team statistics, rotas and new personal targets. But her colleagues reacted badly to the speed of changes and her mentor had a quiet word with her ('Go for "Evolution" not "Revolution".') So Martha slowed down and introduced the changes at a more measured pace, explaining to each colleague in informal one-to-ones why changes were necessary. The result was that her colleagues felt more valued and their self-confidence increased as they successfully navigated the changes.

Assertiveness

Respect is two-way way in a relationship and so it is important that colleagues show respect towards you as well as you showing respect to them. Assertiveness is different from:

- being passive: letting other people treat you badly
- being aggressive: forcefully insisting on your own rights and treating others badly.

Being assertive means that you will:

- respect others' rights as well as your own: be fair to yourself as well as other people
- be proactive rather than reactive; prepare well
- focus on people's behaviour, not criticize them or ignore their identity
- set boundaries
- communicate firmly and confidently.

 TIP *Assert yourself firmly: don't let other people treat you badly and don't insist on your own rights aggressively, treating others badly.*

Saying no to a request

You may find it difficult to say no, perhaps because you want to avoid confrontation or because you want to be liked and appreciated, or you enjoy the feeling of being needed.

- Be aware that others may be trying to make you feel guilty if you were to say no.
- Say no sooner rather than later. Generally speaking, the more you delay something, the more difficult it could become to say no. Be more assertive.
- Work at good relationships (see also Saturday) generally so that you know people well enough that they will not feel offended if you say no.
- Be clear about your own role and priorities. Have these constantly in mind. Is what you are being asked to do a significant distraction from that? If so, then say no.
- Be aware of what you have been trained to do. You may need to refuse to participate in a task or project that you have not been trained for.
- Be aware of your own values. If you are being asked to go beyond those (e.g. if you are asked to lie for your boss), then say no clearly.
- Consider the effects of taking on further tasks. Would undertaking them lead to delays in fulfilling your existing commitments?
- Be reasonable towards yourself: you have a right to say no.
- Practise making such responses as: 'I'd love to help, but I'm already fully committed/stretched.' You could add: 'I hope you find someone else who can help you.' 'I'm fairly busy but if you want to send me a short email letting me know exactly what you want and how you feel I could help, I'll look at it.'
- Suggest an alternative: 'I'm not really sure I'm the right person to deal with this. Why don't you ask ...?'
- If your boss is asking you to take on further responsibilities, put the onus back on them by asking which activity they want you to tackle.
- Discuss what precisely needs to be done.
- Don't apologize; don't say, 'I'll come back to you later if I find I have time', because that adds to your already committed to-do list. Ask your colleague to come back to you later (fortunately, they probably won't). Or you could say, 'You could see if I'm less busy next week.'
- Compromise on what needs to be done; negotiate: 'I'll cover your shift if you do mine on Saturday', but make sure they do so.

Summary

Today we have looked at treating colleagues with respect and have emphasized:

listening to what your colleague is saying to discover the real issue

being sensitive – calm, yet firm – towards your colleague and expressing empathy towards them

asserting yourself by stating the issue and being explicit about your motives

dealing separately with the real issue and the emotions surrounding the issue

remaining polite

being assertive (neither passive nor aggressive)

saying no when appropriate.

Follow-up

1 Think about a difficult conversation at work. What more could you do to listen to people's different viewpoints and distinguish the incident from feelings about the incident? What are the next steps for you to undertake?

2 Ask colleagues whether they consider that you remain professional and polite in dealing with difficult conversations. Act on your colleagues' responses.

3 Consider now, in advance, strategies for saying no to requests that you know will come when you return to your work.

SUNDAY MONDAY TUESDAY WEDNESDAY THURSDAY FRIDAY SATURDAY

Questions

1. Treating colleagues with respect in a difficult conversation, even when you disagree with them is:
   a) nice to have ❏
   b) helpful if you like them ❏
   c) vital ❏
   d) unimportant. ❏

2. When a colleague is talking, to show my understanding, I:
   a) nod my head occasionally ❏
   b) keep my head motionless ❏
   c) shake my head strongly ❏
   d) nod my head vigorously every three seconds. ❏

3. I continue listening to my colleague:
   a) until lunchtime ❏
   b) until I really understand what they think is the problem ❏
   c) until I really understand what they feel ❏
   d) until they stop talking. ❏

4. The emotions surrounding an issue are:
   a) real and need to be dealt with if you have time ❏
   b) real and need to be dealt with, so I make time ❏
   c) so significant that they become the issue and never get resolved ❏
   d) unreal so I ignore them. ❏

5. Showing your understanding for what a colleague is going through is:
   a) a waste of time and energy ❏
   b) nice if that is in your personality ❏
   c) a sign of weakness ❏
   d) important. ❏

6. After discovering the core issue and emotions around the issue, you:
   a) can go home because you have finished the conversation ❏
   b) need to tackle only the emotions ❏
   c) need to respond clearly to both the emotions and the issue ❏
   d) need to tackle only the issue. ❏

7. Apologizing for a genuine error is:
   a) always wrong ❏
   b) sometimes necessary ❏
   c) a waste of time ❏
   d) unhelpful. ❏

8. Being assertive means:
   a) letting things happen and reacting to them ❏
   b) that you will prepare well for a difficult conversation ❏
   c) letting other people tell you what to do ❏
   d) forcefully communicating your point of view to make people accept it. ❏

9. Being assertive means:
a) respecting yourself as well as others ☐
b) being reactive ☐
c) communicating weakly ☐
d) being aggressive. ☐

10. When colleagues ask me to take on even more work:
a) I refuse loudly and angrily ☐
b) I always accept, because I like to help them ☐
c) I always say no, because it is their job ☐
d) I sometimes say no to respect my own rights. ☐

SUNDAY MONDAY TUESDAY WEDNESDAY THURSDAY FRIDAY SATURDAY

FRIDAY

Seek change

Introduction

As we move closer to the end of our week, we now look at some specific examples of difficult conversations. We're building on what we have discussed so far about:

- realizing that you need to tackle difficult conversations rather than avoiding them
- managing your own emotions and those of your colleague
- reframing an issue to look at it in a fresh, positive way
- preparing well for your difficult conversation both in terms of the venue, layout of the room, etc., and also your opening words
- listening carefully to discover the core issue
- treating your colleague with respect
- discerning your colleague's point of view and intentions
- working creatively on possible solutions
- focusing on the goal.

Today we continue to consider your need to be assertive, expressing your viewpoint firmly in a range of situations. Finally, we consider the need to summarize the actions that have been agreed at the end of the conversation so that the whole time has not been wasted.

Performance management

Most companies and organizations have certain procedures in place to consider colleagues' performance. Such procedures, usually included in your Employees' Handbook, are commonly known as performance management, but other terms such as 'performance appraisal' or 'coaching development' are also used.

Appraisals

In an appraisal, a manager meets regularly (e.g. yearly or twice per year) with a member of their team to discuss that colleague's work. In particular, the manager will consider the colleague's:

● performance since the last review. What has gone well? What evidence can they show to demonstrate this? Have the goals that were set then been fulfilled? If not, why not?
● possible future development needs. What areas is the colleague weak in and do they need further training? What skills does the colleague need to develop to enable them to make progress in their career? You may gather information about a colleague's work from other individuals they work with or for, such as fellow team members, subordinates or customers, which is known as 360-degree appraisal. Note that 360-degree appraisal also means that senior managers are appraised by those who work for them.

The general tone of an appraisal is important: I was taught to follow the 'high-low-high' method – begin and end with praise and commendation and sandwich in between discussion of an area that has not gone well. A key aim is to get the colleague who is being appraised to talk most of the time. Listen to your colleague's explanation of such an aspect of their work – there may be certain mitigating factors that have affected it. Remain fair, positive and constructive and tackle weak performance by identifying causes and pursuing appropriate remedies. Your company will have in place certain procedures, for example, capability policy/procedures, if required standards have not been met on a long-term basis.

An appraisal should end by setting objectives. These objectives should be SMART; look back at Tuesday for more details on this.

Making appraisals less difficult

Jack and his colleagues hated the yearly appraisal – the dreaded annual review – so he and his colleagues suggested each member of staff should meet with their boss for an informal one-to-one every month.

The informal one-to-ones meant that difficult issues could be identified earlier and tackled much more quickly before they became serious. For example, Julie's boss saw that she was really struggling with not only her own workload but also that of a colleague who was on long-term sick leave, so her boss was able to bring in help more quickly. And Peter had been on a really helpful report-writing course, the results of which his boss asked him to pass on to others at their staff meeting. The introduction of one-to-ones meant that relations between colleagues and managers were better, managers were much better informed about their staff and annual appraisals became far less unpleasant.

The limits of change

Before we look at a range of situations, we need to consider a more general matter: you can change yourself but you cannot change other people.

We can hope our colleague will change, but we cannot actually make the changes for them.

We can persuade and try to convince them of the need to change, but that may not be effective. What I have been trying to show in this book is that involving someone in a conversation in which they and their views are listened to and respected is far more likely to lead them to change their own behaviour and actions.

Engage your colleague in the conversation

Because you treat your colleague with respect and allow them to share their emotions and intentions and because you make the assumptions explicit that you are working towards, you can engage your colleague in resolving the issue.

One way is to ask them, 'What do you think you should do?' or, 'What options do you think are open to you (us)?' Asking such a question may open up fruitful lines of enquiry. Such an approach is far better than you telling them directly what you think they should do. Involving them further also deepens the trust you have in them and allows them to take responsibility.

Make sure your question is not expressed in a threatening tone and also that it is directed towards resolving the issue. (See also Wednesday on asking questions.)

So if a colleague is always late for work, don't say to them, 'So when will you start getting to work on time?', which will probably result in a sullen 'I don't know.' Instead ask, 'What do you think you should do?' or 'What options do you think are open to you?' This may open up a conversation on other issues in their life such as childcare or looking after elderly relatives, which might in turn lead to discussing alternative working methods such as shift work or working from home one day per week.

Get your colleague to see the difficulty: don't tell them. Do you remember the story on Sunday? If the manager, John, had told Gary directly and bluntly that he was incompetent, Gary would have become even more defensive than he was. He simply wouldn't have been open to any ideas on a different job. But because John was a wise manager, he respected Gary and encouraged Gary to discuss the parts of his job that he did enjoy. Such discussion provided the basis for arousing Gary's interest in the other role.

When not to deal with a situation

If the matter is minor, then let it go, if it does not create a barrier between you and a colleague. This will mean that you will not keep thinking about it. Further, the matter may be a problem with you, not your colleague. I was on an awayday once and in the open discussion Jane told her colleague Susie that she (Jane) had always had a problem with Susie. That was Jane's problem, but Jane's speaking about it explicitly made Susie feel uncomfortable. Jane need not have said anything to Susie at all. The problem lay with Jane, not Susie.

Specific situations

Giving bad news

The way you handle giving bad news will to some extent depend on your own personality.

- **Begin briefly but definitely**. How do you handle giving other bad news, for example telling other members of the family that someone has died? In our family, I have noticed over time that we have introduced it with a very brief statement such as 'Are you sitting down?', 'I've got some bad news' or 'I'm afraid I've got some bad news.' So it can be helpful to begin briefly but definitely.
- **Give the bad news clearly and directly**. Come to the point quickly; don't be evasive. Say: 'You didn't get the job.' These will be the words that your colleague will remember, so spend time phrasing them carefully: look back at Tuesday for more on this.
- **Allow your colleague to answer**. If they burst into tears, then let them express such emotions (see Monday). If you are telling them they have not got the job they were hoping for, then you could say, 'I realize this is disappointing for you' or something similar if this is appropriate.

- **Bring the conversation to an end in due course**. Because you are well prepared (see Tuesday), you will already know the next steps that your colleague needs to take. For example, there may be papers they need to sign. Or, if appropriate, you could suggest a further meeting at a later date to discuss the next steps.

Receiving criticism

None of us likes to receive criticism, but it is one way in which we learn and grow.

- If the criticism is justified, then thank your colleague and if necessary apologize for having done something wrong (or for not having done something right) and assure them that you will change your behaviour in a similar situation in future.
- If the criticism is not justified, think about what your colleague has said. You may later want to say something like, 'I understand your point of view, Jack, but I think I see things differently from you.' You could then outline your approach, explaining as necessary your intentions and assumptions and then discuss the situation with your colleague to see if there is any common ground that could provide a basis for agreement.

Dealing with lazy, stubborn or unmotivated colleagues

Your aim here is to point out benefits of working harder or more flexibly.

Be specific: encourage them to see their role in the team: 'Entering the data into the computer by 12p.m. allows the rest of the marketing team to work more effectively'. 'If we (note: begin with 'we' not 'you') don't deliver the order to Manchester by Friday, we will probably lose the next contract. So you need to ...'. 'How do you think we should proceed on this issue?' (i.e. giving them the responsibility, not simply asking, 'Have you got any ideas as to how we should proceed on this issue?', which could lead to them answering, 'No').

Dealing with aggressive, negative or selfish colleagues

Sometimes colleagues are bullies or are so critical or selfish that working with them becomes almost intolerable. Different approaches are recommended:

● Point out the effects of their behaviour, for example, 'Because you used abusive language, two colleagues have asked to be moved to a different department'.
● Try not to let their negative emotions affect you. Do all you can to remain calm, although I realize this is difficult to do in practice.
● Try to minimize how much you have to deal directly with this colleague.
● Make the point to your boss that you would work more efficiently elsewhere (i.e. don't make the issue too personal).
● Deal with facts rather than emotions. The kind of person we are describing may well enjoy playing on your emotions. Keep matters objective and logical. Be as unemotional as possible: 'Such comments are unprofessional.' Resist wasting time arguing with such colleagues.

Dealing with an incompetent boss

Some bosses see themselves as very important and perfect and they don't like to think their authority is being undermined. But the reality is that some bosses do not have the knowledge or skills to fulfil their jobs well. In fact, none of us is perfect and no one knows all the answers. So realize that your boss has strengths and weaknesses. Here are some suggested tactics:

● Point out errors indirectly. At times it may be appropriate to say, 'You may not have realized, but ...' or 'I'm sure it was an inadvertent error.' Or you can fill in the gaps in their skill sets in what you do.

- Check your facts are accurate before criticizing them.
- Be positive: 'We can deliver the order to China on time if Kate helps us. Shall I ask her?' rather than, 'We'll miss the deadline to deliver the order to China unless you ask Kate to help us.'
- Discuss the difficulty and possible ways forward with a trusted colleague or friend who will keep the matter confidential.
- Try to avoid being disloyal to your boss when you are with colleagues.
- As a last resort, go to your boss's boss.

Dealing with an angry client

Listen to their complaint – take them seriously. Ask questions to get to the heart of the issue. It can be helpful to put yourself in their position and try to empathize with what they are experiencing (e.g. faulty goods, late delivery, the frustration of waiting 30 minutes on the phone to get through). If you are in a face-to-face meeting, maintain eye contact.

After you have let the other person express their emotion and seen their anger subside, think what you can do.

If there are positive steps you can take, then you could ask something like, 'What can I do to help?' (They may find such a direct question disarming.) At the least, you should think of some positive options that you can offer: 'We can offer you a refund of ...', 'We can give you another night's bed and breakfast free.'

If you can offer at least two alternatives, then this will help them see that they have greater control over the situation than before.

If necessary, apologize in specific cases: 'I'm sorry but in this instance we let you down', but don't be excessive in apologizing; your client will be more concerned with putting matters right.

Dealing with perfectionists

We're not discussing doing a good job here, we're talking about colleagues who are critical to the point of distinguishing between an italic or roman full stop. Such colleagues concentrate on small unimportant details and are also sometimes awkward and inflexible – there seems to be an excessive desire (to the point of obsession) in them to make sure everything is right. They are more interested in the letter of the law than the spirit of the law.

So encourage such a colleague to see the situation as a whole: 'Alice, if you continue to triple-check every cell in the spreadsheet against the data in all the other files, we'll miss the deadline. What do you think you can do to help us meet that deadline?' Notice the positive emphasis of the second sentence; not, 'What do you think you should stop doing to help us meet that deadline?'

Dealing with gossips

Gossip can spread like wildfire. For example, a careless comment about someone's absence can develop into that colleague's full-blown resignation in a matter of minutes.

Ways to deal with gossip include:

- Ignore them. If the matter isn't serious, it will die out quickly.
- Confront them: 'Rupert, was it you who said, "...?"'
- Show that the rumour they passed on is not true; give them the facts: 'The managing director has not resigned.'
- If you cannot say anything, then let people know: 'We're aware there's a rumour going round about ... We're not in a position to say anything at the moment but be assured that we will be able to say more by [state a time].' Of course

it is important that you then keep your promise to give information by that time.

Dealing with shy people

As someone who was shy for many decades, I know it is not helpful to be told directly to 'Stop being shy.' Shy people will become less quiet and reserved when they are ready. So maybe you should put your energies into making the whole situation more relaxed than spending time directing shy people to become less so.

Having said that, you could say to the whole group (not individuals), 'Has anyone else got an opinion they'd like to share?', hoping that the more vocal ones will take the hint not to talk and the quieter ones will see that as permission to express their views.

Dealing with colleagues who resist change

We live in times of great change but many of us prefer to do things in the way in which we have always done them in the past. Your role as manager is, however, to be positive, forward-looking and honest.

● Show your colleagues the goal: where you are heading. The goal may be the same as before, but you are now using a different route to reach it. Take the opportunity to explain that explicitly.

- Explain why you are making the changes ('Company X is now achieving a greater market share than us, and we need to do something to change that').
- Be positive: 'How can we as a company help you?' (not: 'What problems have you got with the proposed changes?').
- Use 'we' statements, not 'you' statements (see previous example).
- Give examples: 'Another company tried this formula, and was very successful. In fact, their profits are three times what they were five years ago.'
- Discuss how the changes will affect them. Emphasize any benefits. Colleagues like – and need – to know the benefits that are in it for them: 'We're relocating the four offices over the next year. We'll be moving to bigger offices so you'll have much more space. We'll be the third office to move, in about June.'

Dealing with inappropriate behaviour or personal hygiene

- Document what happened in a factual record.
- If a colleague has been sexually harassed or racially abused, then discuss this with your HR department immediately.
- Mention the matter in a general way: 'Several colleagues have commented that they find your vocabulary insulting. At [name of] company, we treat one another in a professional way and we would be grateful if you could stop using such language.' 'Some colleagues have become aware of an odour near where you were working.'

When a difficult conversation reaches an impasse, it is sometimes worth going to mediation, which is a different type of conversation. If it goes that far, both parties have to go to mediation genuinely seeking a solution; otherwise it doesn't work.

Summarize at the end of your conversation

Just as colleagues remember the opening words of a difficult conversation, so they may also remember the final words. Think back to a great time with family, friends or colleagues that may have been spoiled at the end because of something that was said: unfortunately that unpleasant final act may remain in your memory far longer than the pleasant time.

Remember to continue to treat your colleague with respect, not least because they will remain a colleague in a working relationship with you at the end of the difficult conversation. You will want them to feel positive as they leave the conversation as the conversation ends and they leave.

Make sure your colleague knows:

- what they need to stop doing
- what they need to start doing
- how they need to change their actions.

Ensure your goals are SMART:

- **S** Specific, not vague
- **M** Measurable and quantifiable
- **A** Agreed by everyone present
- **R** Realistic, achievable and so will develop and challenge your colleague's skills
- **T** Timed: when are the actions to be completed by?

If the conversation has ended positively and well, you could even also suggest that they help a new colleague who is just starting work.

The end of a difficult conversation is not the time:

- to give a colleague further work: 'While you're here, I wonder if you could just ...'

- to affirm a colleague with praise: 'Yes, we've had a tough half hour's chat but I want you to know that I still really am impressed with your work.'

At the end of the conversation, make sure your colleague knows what they need to stop doing, start doing and how they need to change their actions.

SUNDAY

MONDAY

TUESDAY

WEDNESDAY

THURSDAY

FRIDAY

SATURDAY

Summary

Today we've looked at a range of ways of encouraging colleagues to change. We noted that if you are direct at challenging behaviour then that is unlikely to have the desired effect. A far more effective way is to involve your colleague by:

- engaging them in a conversation
- finding out more about them
- listening to them
- respecting them
- seeking positive ways forward.

We then looked at a variety of situations and noted that sometimes you need to be direct (e.g. when giving bad news), whereas on other occasions you need to be indirect (e.g. discussing personal hygiene).

Generally, you should:

- allow your colleague to respond
- be clear, accurate and objective
- remain professional
- be specific
- involve them as far as you can
- be positive: discuss what benefits something will bring them
- distinguish between facts and emotions

- offer alternatives
- encourage colleagues to see how their work fits into the whole
- bring the conversation to a successful conclusion by summarizing at the end.

Follow-up

Think about difficult colleagues who you work with. How will you deal with them?

Questions

1. We have appraisals:
a) once a year ❏
b) never ❏
c) every two weeks ❏
d) when we remember. ❏

2. Some matters are so insignificant that:
a) I still make an issue out of them because I enjoy being awkward ❏
b) I consider them but don't pursue them ❏
c) I have never noticed anything like that ❏
d) I raise them at every opportunity to delay progress on real issues. ❏

3. In a difficult conversation, you must be:
a) as vague as possible ❏
b) as critical as possible ❏
c) as clear as possible ❏
d) as nice as possible. ❏

4. In a difficult conversation being specific is:
a) unnecessary ❏
b) helpful ❏
c) useful if you think that way ❏
d) a waste of time. ❏

5. In a difficult conversation, you should:
a) speak all the time ❏
b) let your colleague talk all the time ❏
c) avoid the issue ❏
d) involve your colleague. ❏

6. In a difficult conversation, you should discuss:
a) your colleague's holiday plans ❏
b) last night's football ❏
c) the benefits of a particular solution ❏
d) the difficulties of a particular solution. ❏

7. In a difficult conversation offering alternatives is:
a) unnecessary ❏
b) the first thing you should do ❏
c) all right if you can think of any ❏
d) important as you have understood what is going on. ❏

8. In a difficult conversation, you should encourage colleagues to:
a) think about their colleagues' work ❏
b) see their own work better ❏
c) know how their own work fits into your company or organization ❏
d) not think about their own work. ❏

9. At the end of a difficult conversation, you should:
a) not bother to summarize at the end, but just go home ❏
b) summarize only the main issue ❏
c) discuss the emotions one more time ❏
d) summarize the actions that colleagues need to fulfil. ❏

10. In a difficult conversation, you should:
a) know the objective facts ❑
b) discuss only emotions ❑
c) discuss only the facts ❑
d) have no plan at all. ❑

SATURDAY

Build trusting relationships

Introduction

We're coming to the end of our week on dealing with difficult conversations. How do you feel? Raring to go and try out the different principles you have read about? Or are you rather daunted at the prospect of saying the wrong thing? Today we put the theme of difficult conversations into perspective and look at how you can make difficult conversations easier by working at building trusting relationships generally.

If you already have good working relationships, then when difficult conversations arise, you will be better placed to deal with them, because you will already have built up a large reserve of goodwill.

We can also express that idea negatively: bad working relationships – or the absence of good working relationships – will mean that the company or organization will not function well and that difficult conversations will be even more difficult than they need be.

I chose the words in the title of this chapter very carefully: *build* – we can take active steps to cultivate and work at relationships; *trusting* working relationships are ones that are firmly established – which takes time – and are not easily broken.

So today we consider how we can cultivate such strong and trusting working relationships.

Develop your own personal qualities

It might seem strange to begin this chapter with yourself, rather than with your relationship with your colleagues, but instead of pointing out others' weaknesses, it can be good at first to take stock of your own life and stop to think about your own attitudes before considering others.

- Do you have integrity?
  - Are you honest and firm in having strong moral principles that you follow? Are you pretending to be someone you're not? (I'm not thinking here of what perhaps most of us have when we feel inexperienced in a new job and wonder whether we can really cope with its demands. I'm thinking of people who actively deceive others and whose whole lives are hiding the truth from others.)
  - Are you straightforward? Do you avoid making deceptive plans or acting unfairly or dishonestly?
  - Do you work too hastily in order to try to save time or money but in doing so, are you less thorough than you know you should be?
  - Do you have many grand ideas, but they remain only as ideas and you don't intend them to become real?
  - Are you a positive person? In a world where much of our entertainment (e.g. soap operas and crime series) is based on deception, we need to guard what enters our minds and hearts and take control of our thoughts. So where possible, we need to be positive in a negative world. (I'm reminded of the times in my life when I have been writing dictionary entries and have spent days on the letter D, with many negative words beginning *dis-*: *disappoint*, *disconcerting*, *discourteous*, *disloyal*, *dissent*, *distress*. It takes a power from outside of myself to rise above such negative words and live a normal, positive life.)
- Are you trustworthy? You will only inspire trust in others if you yourself are reliable and responsible. If you say you will do something by a certain time, do you do so? (Again,

colleagues will notice if you are constantly late in meeting deadlines and so take that as permission that they can act similarly.)

TIP *You will inspire trust in others only if you yourself are reliable and responsible.*

- How committed are you? On the courses that I lead most of the colleagues who come are very keen but occasionally some attend who are very half-hearted. It then requires a great deal of effort and determination to enable them to see things differently and learn. Are you like that in any way? Just as enthusiasm is contagious, so is a lack of commitment and enthusiasm. Members of your team will immediately sense your lack of commitment and think that if you are not committed then there is no need for them to be either.
- Remain loyal to your boss in public; if you disagree with them, discuss any differences with them in private.
- Apologize when you make mistakes. Reading this chapter might make you think I am perfect! Far from it – ask my wife or my work colleagues! So I have also learnt to apologize when I've made a mistake. A wise older friend once told me: 'It's a strong person who admits their weakness.' I found that helpful because ultimately our work – and lives – isn't about how important we think we are; it's about the kind of people we really are.
- If you are a quieter, more sensitive person, you may need to develop a thick skin, and not be so easily hurt, offended or upset by criticism.
- Know your limitations; ask for help if you find yourself in difficulties and unable to cope. Seek advice from a trusted colleague who will keep confidential what you discuss with them. Hopefully, you will have such a (probably small) circle of such trusted colleagues and friends in whom you can confide.

107

Develop good working relationships with others

- Be visible: invest in building strong working relationships with your colleagues.
- Speak to your colleagues; don't use email all the time. Remember their names. Help them. Pay them genuine compliments. Smile at them. Don't ignore small talk; it builds relationships. Show interest in them. (The test for me is if I can remember the place they've been to on holiday. I'm good at asking where colleagues are going on holiday, but poor at remembering the place.) Such little acts of recognition are significant. Listen to them (look back at Wednesday). Express your appreciation of them.

- Be patient. You are in this for the long haul. It takes time to build trusting relationships. Some of the strong working relationships you are cultivating now could well stay with you throughout your career and your whole life.
- Be clear. I've dealt with colleagues who have been so unclear that decades later I still recall their vagueness. If you are delegating to others, be clear what the task is and when you want them to return the work to you. Communicate your expectations clearly.

- Discourage less; encourage more:
  - Discouragement comes to most of us much more naturally than encouragement. Recently I was at the London station into which my trains normally run and I saw two of the railway officials. I wanted to tackle them about slow trains, but I resisted the temptation because I knew (a) that they are probably doing their best within the limits they have to work with and (b) that if I were to say something it would probably come out in a negative and critical tone, so I decided it was better to say nothing at all.
  - Thinking of words of encouragement is harder than expressing discouragement and may well take time. It is much easier to do nothing. Staying with the railways, at our local station there was recently a 'Meet the Managers' discussion where passengers could discuss their concerns with a manager of the railway company. A noticeboard recorded a summary of the discussions, and in the middle of the complaints one positive comment stood out: 'We think the staff at ... station are lovely', which I then relayed to one of the members of staff at the booking office. My going over to the woman behind the glass at the booking office and saying, 'We think you are lovely,' elicited a smile from her, even at 6.10 in the morning! The point I am making is this: if what you are thinking of saying is discouraging, then think whether you need to say it at all. It's better to put your resources into trying to be encouraging.

TIP *It takes at least five acts of encouragement to balance out one of discouragement.*

- If you want to encourage someone, be specific where you can. So rather than a bland, 'Pam, thank you for all you do', you could say, 'Pam, I thought the way you dealt with ... was very helpful. You were positive and supportive.' Above all, be genuine.

- Work hard at planning what you are going to say, but if the words don't come easily or aren't quite right, say or write them anyway. (Think of the last time someone encouraged you – you probably do not remember the exact words they used but you may recall their action as one that increased your self-esteem, hope or confidence. So even if your words are not completely polished, you could say something like, 'Paul, I'm not very good with words but I thought you did a great job in the way you handled the Mortimer account.' I particularly try to be supportive and encourage colleagues when they share something personal and make themselves vulnerable.

- If you need to learn lessons where things have gone wrong, be positive rather than negative. This means that you should not apportion blame but work out what went wrong.

- At times you will need to be courageous:
  - to admit things haven't worked out as you wished
  - to stand up for what you believe is right
  - to sit down and listen to others.

- Be people-focused, not problem-focused. If your people skills are poor, seek help.

- Engage in 'small talk', conversation about ordinary, relatively unimportant things from a strictly business point of view. When you meet someone for the first time, it's all right to talk about their travel to the venue, the weather, their family, the previous night's football results, holiday plans, etc. Engaging in such conversation helps the actual business run more smoothly than if you did not have it. Share a little of how you see life; ask questions, especially closed questions (ones that can be answered with a straight 'yes' or 'no') to begin with and then move on to some open questions (ones that may begin with 'why', 'how', 'who', 'when', 'where', 'what' and get people talking), but don't give the impression that you are interrogating the other person.

- Be aware of roles. When you meet someone for the first time and they tell you they are for example a dentist, doctor, police officer or accountant, be aware that you will probably then put them into a category of that profession and that you will trust them accordingly. On more on roles within a team, see later today.
- Be aware of colleagues' status and power, but treat each person as a unique individual. For example, if you meet a head teacher for the first time, you may assume they have a lot of authority and you may feel insecure because you have a lower status than they do. But the problem may be more in your perception than in reality. If the head teacher genuinely says to you, 'I'm interested in what you can tell me about ...' you may feel honoured that a person in such a position of authority has asked for your opinion. For me, what is important is valuing each person as unique. I recall a comment about a teacher friend years ago: 'He even talks to the cleaners.' Realize that you can crush someone's sense of identity by belittling them, constantly interrupting them or ignoring them.

TIP *Treat each person as a unique individual.*

- Ensure, as far as it is up to you, that the messages expressed by different departments in your company or organization are consistent, i.e. that they do not contradict one another.
- Put the aims of your company or organization first and make sure you fulfil your own work to the best of your capabilities. In most organizations there will be office

politics and you will find people you like and others you don't like. Part of doing your job professionally is rising above, as far as you can, any different outlooks that colleagues have and their diverse personalities. Always be polite; don't engage in gossip. You may need to stop complaining about your colleagues and make sure you do your own work as professionally as possible.

● Recognize colleagues' achievements. Even saying, 'Thank you, you did that well' is an acknowledgement of gratitude. Publicly affirm and recognize colleagues' achievements, i.e. praise colleagues' work in front of others. Bring in food or buy each of them little treats, such as chocolate. Issue certificates for achievements: it's amazing how competitive colleagues can be for a certificate.

Accepting criticism

Andy was just beginning to work as a trainer. He had a great knowledge of his subject, but there was some concern about whether he could communicate his ideas clearly. Peter, a senior colleague, watched him lead a training session and sure enough some areas of weakness became obvious.

At the end of the training session, Peter took Andy aside for a quiet word. Andy was OK about this: it was a safe place. Andy accepted Peter's constructive criticism, because he knew that Peter had his best interests at heart; they had known each other for years.

We can accept constructive criticism from others when we know they have greater knowledge and experience and we trust their motives.

Develop strong teamwork

As team leader, you are responsible for encouraging your team. How can you encourage members of your team to work together successfully?

- Communicate a vision. Where is the team going? What is its purpose? You need to present a strong and inspiring vision of your goals.
- Set clear goals for your team. There is nothing like an abstract statement that is not earthed in reality to turn people off. It is hardly surprising that colleagues come out of a team meeting feeling cynical when a vision has been cast but no practical implications have been drawn from that vision. A vision must be turned into practical steps.
- Remember that a team is essentially a group of people, not skills, agendas or problems.
- Know that the strength of the team comes from a combination of strengths (see www.belbin.com for further help on this).
- Ensure your values as a team are agreed. Do team members trust and respect one another? Do individuals feel important and part of something bigger than themselves? Encourage team members to remain positive, to believe in the strength and unity of the team.
- Clarify the responsibilities of each member of the team so that not only each individual knows their responsibilities but also the whole team knows what each member does. Different members of the team will bring different skills, so play to colleagues' strengths. For example, don't give the chair of a meeting to someone who is unclear or indecisive.
- Try to assign work to colleagues that suits their passion and skills, so that you get the best out of them. If colleagues are clearly in the wrong job, encourage them to think laterally as to where their skills could best be applied.
- Ensure lines of authority and responsibility are clear. Be clear about whether individual team members have authority to spend sums of money over a certain amount. Or should they direct all requests for purchases through you as team leader?
- Be flexible about what is negotiable and different styles of working. Listen to suggestions from your colleagues. Be prepared to 'think outside the box' to creatively challenge existing patterns of thinking and working and find solutions to difficulties.

- Be fair and treat all your colleagues equally, even though you may like some more than others.
- Make sure each team member works as hard as every other one: each is to fulfil their responsibilities. You cannot afford to have colleagues in your team who work significantly less than others.
- Encourage openness. As far as you can, involve members of the team in making decisions. Bring out those who are shy and use your skills of diplomacy to quieten those who talk too much.
- Encourage team members to use their initiative. They do not always need to come back to you to solve small difficulties but can be enterprising and resolve issues themselves.
- Encourage colleagues to look out for one another, so that, for example, where one colleague is struggling, a fellow team member can step in and help them.
- Challenge the team to work even more effectively. Don't encourage them to sit back but be constantly on the lookout for better ways of doing things that reduce time or money. For example, are team members entering the same data into two different spreadsheets? Combine them into one, so that a colleague need input the figures only once.
- Set in place effective monitoring controls to track what you are doing and then evaluate your progress regularly. For example, if you find that staff expenses claims are not being properly checked, then you must act on this promptly.
- Celebrate success. Recognize the success of individuals. In some cultures colleagues are shy or embarrassed about doing this, but it is an important part of valuing and appreciating people. Celebrate team success: if you have completed a project, go out and mark the occasion by doing something different, such as having a special lunch or an evening meal. Such times help develop a sense of belonging to a team.

TIP *Celebrate success. Recognize the success of individuals and of the team as a whole.*

- Give feedback. You as team leader should give informal feedback to team members on whether they are doing well ... or not so well. Be specific (e.g. 'I thought the tone of your email in response to the complaint was excellent'); encourage accountability and deal with difficulties sooner rather than later so they do not become serious.
- Provide opportunities for members of your team to approach you if they need help. You should not be aloof.
- Provide opportunities for training colleagues, particularly in areas that have been shown in appraisals and reviews as needing further development.
- Encourage fun. Hold team-building days where you deliberately mix people up into different groups from those they are normally in. Set tasks in which the groups compete against one another. The resulting banter will produce laughter and make people relaxed with one another and you will see sides of people that you have not seen before.

Working at a relationship

Peter started working at a new company. From the day of his interview, he'd been warned about a colleague, Derek, as someone who was very awkward and difficult to work with. Peter introduced himself to Derek immediately on his first day and commented that his job must be demanding and how pressurized his role must be, with many colleagues making demands on him and his time. Peter went on to ask for Derek's help in a project he knew he would be working on and ended by saying that he looked forward to working with him.

Colleagues expressed surprise at how well Peter worked with Derek but it all began with Peter working hard at building a good relationship with Derek and treating him with respect.

Summary

Today we've looked at practical ways in which you as a manager can build strong, trustworthy relationships with colleagues. This is good to do, not only to help you through the difficult times that will inevitably come, but also because it is good in itself.

SUNDAY MONDAY TUESDAY WEDNESDAY THURSDAY FRIDAY SATURDAY

Follow-up

1 Look at the following list of qualities:

- ability to accept criticism
- ability to apologize
- clarity when delegating
- commitment
- courage
- encouraging others
- enthusiasm
- expressing appreciation of colleagues
- good communicator
- good listening skills
- good team leader
- integrity
- knowing your limits
- loyalty
- patience
- reliability

2 Which three qualities are you strong at?

3 Which three qualities do you need to develop more?

4 What practical steps can you take to cultivate the three qualities you need to develop more? What specifically can you do and when can you do it?

SUNDAY
MONDAY
TUESDAY
WEDNESDAY
THURSDAY
FRIDAY
SATURDAY

Questions

1. Building trusting working relationships in an organization is:
   a) a luxury ❑
   b) essential ❑
   c) a waste of time ❑
   d) unimportant. ❑

2. In trying to build better relationships, you should think more about:
   a) discouraging others ❑
   b) encouraging others ❑
   c) your boss ❑
   d) your holidays. ❑

3. 'Small talk' is:
   a) a useful tool to establish rapport ❑
   b) a complete waste of time ❑
   c) more important than the actual business ❑
   d) just about adequate. ❑

4. When thinking about others' roles:
   a) I am awed by those with higher status ❑
   b) I am very bossy towards those with lower status ❑
   c) I have this at the back of my mind but don't let it control me ❑
   d) I don't think about others. ❑

5. In our team, we are clear about having:
   a) strictly defined roles that we discuss whenever we meet ❑
   b) different roles that we use as a basis to help us ❑
   c) no set roles at all ❑
   d) all the same roles. ❑

6. I'd like to improve teamwork in my team:
   a) our teamwork is fine thank you; I don't need to do anything more ❑
   b) and I'm keen to take practical action to do so ❑
   c) but I'm so aware of my failings as team leader ❑
   d) but I'm too lazy to do anything about it. ❑

7. In giving work to colleagues:
   a) I just give work to colleagues, regardless of their skills and experience ❑
   b) I don't delegate or give work to colleagues; that's why I feel I'm indispensable and I'm overworked ❑
   c) on a good day, I try to be clear about the work I delegate ❑
   d) I try to find work that suits their passion and skills. ❑

8. If someone is at fault, I:
   a) ignore it and move on, hoping it won't happen again ❑
   b) point it out to them in public, so that the embarrassment will stay with them throughout their career ❑
   c) ignore it, not bothering to learn lessons for next time ❑
   d) have a quiet word with them in private. ❑

9. In celebrating success, I:
a) publicly acknowledge individuals' strengths ❑
b) have a quiet word with the individual so that they don't become too proud and the rest of the team don't know about it ❑
c) half-heartedly and unwillingly acknowledge others' strengths ❑
d) I'm too shy to do this, so I don't. ❑

10. I'm focused on:
a) solving problems ❑
b) tackling crises ❑
c) developing people to fulfil their potential ❑
d) myself. ❑

How to thrive in a tough economic climate

During an economic recession, difficult conversations may occur more often as everyone feels the squeeze. Colleagues may be more stressed as they are hanging on to their jobs in an increasingly competitive environment where fewer jobs are available. But don't be discouraged! If you remember what you've read in this book, you will be able to do everything possible to make those difficult conversations easier.

Here are ten crucial tips to help you make sure your conversations remain professional in tough times:

1 Communicate effectively

During an economic recession, good business communication becomes even more important. Organizations that recognize that effective communication is essential for business are more likely to survive and prosper than those that don't. Managers in organizations that value communication know that strong working relationships help morale in the company and make the organization run more smoothly. The advantage is that when – and it is when not if – difficult conversations occur, there is a reserve of goodwill among colleagues that makes the conversations less difficult.

2 Value your employees

Those organizations that value their people create a culture that enables them not only to survive but also to adapt in tough economic times. Begin today by motivating, encouraging and affirming colleagues. As a manager, your role is not only to treat colleagues with respect but also to put in place steps so that everyone can achieve their full potential.

3 Be clear

In tough economic times, you will be even more aware that 'time is money' and you will want to make the most of every conversation, so you will do your best to be clear – in your aims for a conversation, in appraisals, in the outcomes you are seeking from a conversation. You will want to avoid vague generalities, and so will be focused and prepare well for conversations to avoid wasting time and resources. You will come to a meeting with clearly thought-through creative solutions as the way forward. If a conversation is being sidetracked you will steer it back on track.

4 Remain professional

In a recession, you may have more difficult conversations than usual. Make sure you think through what you want to say, especially the opening words of a difficult conversation. Do not give in to the temptation not to prepare well. Realize you need to tackle issues, not ignore them hoping they will go away. Don't put off dealing with the difficult issues. Be professional and firm and fair.

5 Be a good listener

You will know that listening is at the heart of winning through a difficult conversation. You will know that you need to listen until you get to the heart of a problem. This may be more difficult in tough times because other matters may be apparent and you will need to discern the significant underlying issue.

6 Be assertive

Being assertive is the midway point between being passive and being aggressive. If your character is to be more passive and gentle, your role as manager may mean you have to be firm at times. If necessary, push yourself in difficult conversations to be more forceful than you are naturally. If you are naturally a very confident personality, you may need to learn to be less forceful in order to get the best out of people.

7 Be diplomatic

Because you will want to get the best out of people, you will at times have a quiet word with someone in private. You will know when to raise and deal with an issue and when it is not significant and you can let it go.

8 Know how to say no

In tough economic times, with fewer staff, the pressure may be on you to take on more than you can reasonably handle. You will at times have to say no to your colleagues simply to survive and complete your own work; look back for suggestions on how to do this on Thursday.

9 Be positive

In the economic downturn, there is a lot of bad news around. Do your best to be a positive, constructive team leader. Rise above the general negativity and cynicism around you and don't settle for doing nothing. Emphasize benefits and alternative options whenever you can, giving a strong, positive lead.